AF450218

THE SCARECROW

LECTOR HOUSE PUBLIC DOMAIN WORKS

This book is a result of an effort made by Lector House towards making a contribution to the preservation and repair of original classic literature. The original text is in the public domain in the United States of America, and possibly other countries depending upon their specific copyright laws.

In an attempt to preserve, improve and recreate the original content, certain conventional norms with regard to typographical mistakes, hyphenations, punctuations and/or other related subject matters, have been corrected upon our consideration. However, few such imperfections might not have been rectified as they were inherited and preserved from the original content to maintain the authenticity and construct, relevant to the work. We believe that this work holds historical, cultural and/or intellectual importance in the literary works community, therefore despite the oddities, we accounted the work for print as a part of our continuing effort towards preservation of literary work and our contribution towards the development of the society as a whole, driven by our beliefs.

We are grateful to our readers for putting their faith in us and accepting our imperfections with regard to preservation of the historical content. We shall strive hard to meet up to the expectations to improve further to provide an enriching reading experience.

Though, we conduct extensive research in ascertaining the status of copyright before redeveloping a version of the content, in rare cases, a classic work might be incorrectly marked as not-in-copyright. In such cases, if you are the copyright holder, then kindly contact us or write to us, and we shall get back to you with an immediate course of action.

HAPPY READING!

THE SCARECROW

PERCY MACKAYE

ISBN: 978-93-5336-039-9

First Published: 1911

© LECTOR HOUSE LLP

LECTOR HOUSE LLP
E-MAIL: lectorpublishing@gmail.com

THE SCARECROW
OR
THE GLASS OF TRUTH
A TRAGEDY OF THE LUDICROUS

BY

PERCY MACKAYE

NEW YORK
THE MACMILLAN COMPANY
1911

All rights reserved

**COPYRIGHT, 1908,
BY THE MACMILLAN COMPANY.**

*Set up and electrotyped.
Published February, 1908.
Reprinted February, 1911.*

This play has been copyrighted and published simultaneously in the United States and Great Britain. All acting rights, both professional and amateur, are reserved in the United States, Great Britain, and countries of the Copyright Union, by Percy MacKaye. Performances forbidden and right of representation reserved. Application for the right of performing this piece must be made to The McMillan Company. Any piracy or infringement will be prosecuted in accordance with the penalties provided by the United States Statutes: —

"Sec. 4966. — Any person publicly performing or representing any dramatic or musical composition, for which copyright has been obtained, without the consent of the proprietor of the said dramatic or musical composition, or his heirs or assigns, shall be liable for damages therefor, such damages in all cases to be assessed at such sum, not less than one hundred dollars for the first and fifty dollars for every subsequent performance, as to the Court shall appear to be just. If the unlawful performance and representation be wilful and for profit, such person or persons shall be guilty of a misdemeanor, and upon conviction be imprisoned for a period not exceeding one year." U. S. Revised Statutes, Title 60, Chap. 3.

Norwood Press
J. S. Cushing Co. — Berwick & Smith Co.
Norwood, Mass., U.S.A.

TO
MY MOTHER
IN MEMORY OF AUSPICIOUS
"COUNTINGS OF THE CROWS"
BY OLD NEW ENGLAND CORN-FIELDS

PREFACE

But for a fantasy of Nathaniel Hawthorne, this play, of course, would never have been written. In "Mosses from an Old Manse," the *Moralized Legend* "Feathertop" relates, in some twenty pages of its author's inimitable style, how Mother Rigby, a reputed witch of old New England days, converted a corn-patch scarecrow into the semblance of a fine gentleman of the period; how she despatched this semblance to "play its part in the great world, where not one man in a hundred, she affirmed, was gifted with more real substance than itself"; how there the scarecrow, while paying court to pretty Polly Gookin, the rosy, simpering daughter of Justice Gookin, discovered its own image in a looking-glass, returned to Mother Rigby's cottage, and dissolved into its original elements.

My indebtedness, therefore, to this source, in undertaking the present play, goes without saying. Yet it would not be true, either to Hawthorne's work or my own, to classify "The Scarecrow" as a dramatization of "Feathertop." Were it intended to be such, the many radical departures from the conception and the treatment of Hawthorne which are evident in the present work would have to be regarded as so many unwarrantable liberties taken with its original material; the function of the play itself would, in such case, become purely formal, —translative of a narrative to its appropriate dramatic form, —and as such, however interesting and commendable an effort, would have lost all *raison d'être* for the writer.

But such, I may say, has not been my intention. My aim has been quite otherwise. Starting with the same basic theme, I have sought to elaborate it, by my own treatment, to a different and more inclusive issue.

Without particularizing here the full substance of Hawthorne's consummate sketch, which is available to every reader, the divergence I refer to may be summed up briefly.

The scarecrow Feathertop of Hawthorne is the imaginative epitome or symbol of human charlatanism, with special emphasis upon the coxcombry of fashionable society. In his essential superficiality he is characterized as a fop, "strangely self-satisfied," with "nobby little nose thrust into the air." "And many a fine gentleman," says Mother Rigby, "has a pumpkin-head as well as my scarecrow." His hollow semblance is the shallowness of a "well-digested conventionalism, which had incorporated itself thoroughly with his substance and transformed him into a work of art." "But the clothes in this case were to be the making of the man," and so Mother Rigby, after fitting him out in a suit of embroidered finery, endows him as a finishing touch "with a great deal of brass, which she applied to his forehead, thus making it yellower than before. 'With that brass alone,' quoth she, 'thou canst pay thy way all over the earth.'"

Similarly, the other characters are sketched by Hawthorne in accord with this general conception. Pretty Polly Gookin, "tossing her head and managing her fan" before the mirror, views therein "an unsubstantial little maid that reflected every gesture and did all the foolish things that Polly did, but without making her ashamed of them. In short, it was the fault of pretty Polly's ability, rather than her will, if she failed to be as complete an artifice as the illustrious Feathertop himself."

Thus the *Moralized Legend* reveals itself as a satire upon a restricted artificial phase of society. As such, it runs its brief course, with all the poetic charm and fanciful suggestiveness of our great New Englander's prose style, to its appropriate *dénouement*,—the disintegration of its hero.

"'My poor, dear, pretty Feathertop,' quoth Mother Rigby, with a rueful glance at the relics of her ill-fated contrivance, 'there are thousands upon thousands of coxcombs and charlatans in the world made up of just such a jumble of worn-out, forgotten, and good-for-nothing trash as he was, yet they live in fair repute and never see themselves for what they are. And why should my poor puppet be the only one to know himself and perish for it?'"

Coxcombry and charlatanism, then, are the butt of Hawthorne's satire in his *Legend*. The nature of his theme, however, is susceptible of an application far less restricted, a development far more universal, than such satire. This wider issue once or twice in his sketch he seems to have touched upon, only immediately to ignore again. Thus, in the very last paragraph, Mother Rigby exclaims: "Poor Feathertop! I could easily give him another chance and send him forth again to-morrow. But no! *His feelings are too tender—his sensibilities too deep.*"

In these words, spoken in irony, Hawthorne ends his narrative with an undeveloped aspect of his theme, which constitutes the starting-point of the conception of my play: the aspect, namely, of the essential *tragedy of the ludicrous*; an aspect which, in its development, inevitably predicates for my play a divergent treatment and a different conclusion. The element of human sympathy is here substituted for that of irony, as criterion of the common absurdity of mankind.

The scarecrow Feathertop is ridiculous, as the emblem of a superficial fop; the scarecrow Ravensbane is pitiful, as the emblem of human bathos.

Compared with our own ideas of human perfection, what human rubbish we are! Of what incongruous elements are we constructed by time and inheritance wherewith to realize the reasonableness, the power, the altruism, of our dreams! What absurdity is our highest consummation! Yet the sense of our common deficiency is, after all, our salvation. *There* is one reality which is a basic hope for the realization of those dreams. This sense is human sympathy, which is, it would seem, a more searching critic of human frailty than satire. It is the growth of this sense which dowers with dignity and reality the hollowest and most ludicrous of mankind, and becomes in such a fundamental grace of character. In a recent critical interpretation of Cervantes' great work, Professor G. E. Woodberry writes: "A madman has no character; but it is the character of Don Quixote that at last draws the knight out of all his degradations and makes him triumph in the heart of the reader." And he continues: "Modern dismay begins in the thought that here is not the abnormality of an individual, but the madness of the soul in its own nature."

If for "madness" in this quotation I may be permitted to substitute *ludicrousness* (or *incongruity*), a more felicitous expression of my meaning, as applied to Ravensbane in this play, would be difficult to devise.

From what has been said, it will, I trust, be the more clearly apparent why "The Scarecrow" cannot with any appropriateness be deemed a dramatization of "Feathertop," and why its manifold divergencies from the latter in treatment and motive cannot with any just significance be considered as liberties taken with an original source. Dickon, for example, whose name in the *Legend* is but a momentary invocation in the mouth of Mother Rigby, becomes in my play not merely the characterized visible associate of Goody Rickby ("Blacksmith Bess"), but the necessary foil of sceptical irony to the human growth of the scarecrow. So, too, for reasons of the play's different intent, Goody Rickby herself is differentiated from Mother Rigby; and Rachel Merton has no motive, of character or artistic design, in common with pretty, affected Polly Gookin.

My indebtedness to the New England master in literature is, needless to say, gratefully acknowledged; but it is fitting, I think, to distinguish clearly between the aim and the scope of "Feathertop" and that of the play in hand, as much in deference to the work of Hawthorne as in comprehension of the spirit of my own.

P. M-K.

Cornish, New Hampshire,

December, 1907.

Program of the play as first performed in
New York, Jan. 17, 1911, at the Garrick Theatre

CHARLES FROHMAN, MANAGER

HENRY B. HARRIS PRESENTS

EDMUND BREESE

—AS—

THE DEVIL

—IN—

THE SCARECROW

A FANTASTIC ROMANCE   BY PERCY MACKAYE

CHARACTERS

(NOTE—The following characters are named is the order in which they first appear)

BLACKSMITH BESS (Goody Rickby)	ALICE FISCHER
DICKON, a Yankee Improvisation of the Prince of Darkness	EDMUND BREESE
RACHEL MERTON, niece of the Justice	FOLA LA FOLLETTE
RICHARD TALBOT	EARLE BROWNE
JUSTICE GILEAD MERTON	BRIGHAM ROYCE
LORD RAVENSBANE (The Scarecrow)	FRANK REICHER
MISTRESS CYNTHIA MERTON, sister of the Justice	MRS. FELIX MORRIS
MICAH, a servant	HAROLD M. CHESHIRE
CAPTAIN BUGBY, the Governor's secretary	REGAN HUGHSTON
MINISTER DODGE	CLIFFORD LEIGH
MISTRESS DODGE, his wife	ELEANOR SHELDON
REV. MASTER RAND, of Harvard College	WILLIAM LEVIS
REV. MASTER TODD, of Harvard College	HARRY LILLFORD

Sir Charles Reddington, Lieutenant Governor ... H. J. Carvill

Mistress Reddington } his ... Zenaidee Williams

Amelia Reddington } daughters ... Georgia Dvorak

Time—About 1690   Place—A town in Massachusetts

Act I.—The Blacksmith Shop of "Blacksmith Bess." Dawn.
Acts II., III., and IV.—Justice Merton's Parlor.

Morning, afternoon, and evening.

Produced under the direction of Edgar Selwyn

Incidental and entre'act music by Robert Hood Bowers

The portrait of Justice Merton, as a young man,
by John W. Alexander

Scenery designed and painted by H. Robert Law
Costumes by Darian, from designs by Byron Nestor

All of the music composed especially for this production,
by ROBERT HOOD BOWERS

Overture—Devil's Motif; Hymn; Love Motif; Ravensbane's Minuet, etc.

First Entre'act—Ravensbane goes a-wooing. He is instructed in the art by the Devil. He aspires to Rachel's hand.

Second Entre'act—The challenge to the duel. The squire sends his second, the town dandy, to wait upon Ravensbane.

Third Entre'act—Ravensbane's crow song with its tragic ending. His despair.

CONTENTS

DRAMATIS PERSONÆ

- JUSTICE GILEAD MERTON.

- GOODY RICKBY ("Blacksmith Bess").

- LORD RAVENSBANE ("Marquis of Oxford, Baron of *Wittenberg, Elector of Worms, and Count of Cordova*"), *their hypothetical son.*

- DICKON, *a Yankee improvisation of the Prince of Darkness.*

- RACHEL MERTON, *niece of the Justice.*

- MISTRESS CYNTHIA MERTON, *sister of the Justice.*

- RICHARD TALBOT, *Esquire, betrothed to Rachel.*

- SIR CHARLES REDDINGTON, *Lieutenant Governor.*

- MISTRESS REDDINGTON } *his*

- AMELIA REDDINGTON   } *daughters.*

- CAPTAIN BUGBY, *the Governor's Secretary.*

- MINISTER DODGE.

- MISTRESS DODGE, *his wife.*

- REV. MASTER RAND, *of Harvard College.*

- REV. MASTER TODD, *of Harvard College.*

- MICAH, *a servant of the Justice.*

TIME.—*Late Seventeenth Century.*

PLACE.—*A town in Massachusetts.*

ACT I

The interior of a blacksmith shop. Right centre, a forge. Left, a loft, from which are hanging dried cornstalks, hay, and the yellow ears of cattle-corn. Back centre, a wide double door, closed when the curtain rises. Through this door—when later it is opened—is visible a New England landscape in the late springtime: a distant wood; stone walls, high elms, a well-sweep; and, in the near foreground, a ploughed field, from which the green shoots of early corn are just appearing. The blackened walls of the shop are covered with a miscellaneous collection of old iron, horseshoes, cart wheels, etc., the usual appurtenances of a smithy. In the right-hand corner, however, is an array of things quite out of keeping with the shop proper: musical instruments, puppets, tall clocks, and fantastical junk. Conspicuous amongst these articles is a large standing mirror, framed grotesquely in old gold and curtained by a dull stuff, embroidered with peaked caps and crescent moons.

Just before the scene opens, a hammer is heard ringing briskly upon steel. As the curtain rises there is discovered, standing at the anvil in the flickering light of a bright flame from the forge, a woman—powerful, ruddy, proud with a certain masterful beauty, white-haired (as though prematurely), bare-armed to the elbows, clad in a dark skirt (above her ankles), a loose blouse, open at the throat; a leathern apron and a workman's cap. The woman is GOODY RICKBY. On the anvil she is shaping a piece of iron. Beside her stands a framework of iron formed like the ribs and backbone of a man. For a few moments she continues to ply her hammer, amid a shower of sparks, till suddenly the flame on the forge dies down.

GOODY RICKBY Dickon! More flame.

A VOICE [*Above her.*] Yea, Goody. [*The flame in the forge spurts up high and suddenly.*]

GOODY RICKBY Nay, not so fierce.

THE VOICE [*At her side.*] Votre pardon, madame. [*The flame subsides.*] Is that better?

GOODY RICKBY That will do. [*With her tongs, she thrusts the iron into the flame; it turns white-hot.*] Quick work; nothing like brimstone for the smithy trade.

[*At the anvil, she begins to weld the iron rib on to the framework.*]

There, my beauty! We'll make a stout set of ribs for you. I'll see to it this year that I have a scarecrow can outstand all the nor'easters that blow. I've no notion to lose my corn-crop this summer.

[*Outside, the faint cawings of crows are heard. Putting down her tongs and hammer, Goody Rickby strides to the double door, and flinging it wide open, lets in the gray light of dawn. She looks out over the fields and shakes her fist.*]

So ye're up before me and the sun, are ye? [*Squinting against the light.*] There's one! Nay, two. Aha! One for sorrow, Two for mirth— Good! This time we'll have the laugh on our side. [*She returns to the forge, where again the fire has died out.*] Dickon! Fire! Come, come, where be thy wits?

THE VOICE [*Sleepily from the forge.*] 'Tis early, dame.

GOODY RICKBY The more need— [*Takes up her tongs.*]

THE VOICE [*Screams.*] Ow!

GOODY RICKBY Ha! Have I got thee?

[*From the blackness of the forge she pulls out with her tongs, by the right ear, the figure of a devil, horned and tailed. In general aspect, though he resembles a mediæval familiar demon, yet the suggestions of a goatish beard, a shrewdly humorous smile, and (when he speaks) the slightest of nasal drawls, remotely simulate a species of Yankee rustic. Goody Rickby substitutes her fingers for the tongs.*]

Now, Dickon!

DICKON *Deus!* I haven't been nabbed like that since St. Dunstan tweaked my nose. Well, sweet Goody?

GOODY RICKBY The bellows!

DICKON [*Going slowly to the forge.*] Why, 'tis hardly dawn yet. Honest folks are still abed. It makes a long day.

GOODY RICKBY [*Working, while Dickon plies the bellows.*] Aye, for your black pets, the crows, to work in. That's why I'm at it early. You heard 'em. We must have this scarecrow of ours out in the field at his post before sunrise. [*Finishing.*] So, there! Now, Dickon boy, I want that you should—

DICKON [*Whipping out a note-book and writing.*] Wait! Another one! "I want that you should—"

GOODY RICKBY What's that you're writing?

DICKON The phrase, Goody dear; the construction. Your New England dialect is hard for a poor cosmopolitan devil. What with *ut* clauses in English and Latinized subjunctives—You want that I should—Well?

GOODY RICKBY Make a masterpiece. I've made the frame strong, so as to stand the weather; *you* must make the body lifelike so as to fool the crows. Last year I stuck up a poor sham and after a day they saw through it. This time, we must make 'em think it's a real human crittur.

DICKON To fool the philosophers is my specialty, but the crows—hm!

GOODY RICKBY Pooh! That staggers thee!

DICKON Madame Rickby, prod not the quick of my genius. I am Phidias, I am Raphael, I am the Lord God!— You shall see— [*Demands with a gesture.*] Yonder broomstick.

GOODY RICKBY [*Fetching him a broom from the corner.*] Good boy!

DICKON [*Straddling the handle.*] Haha! gee up! my Salem mare. [*Then, pseudo-philosophically.*] A broomstick—that's for imagination!

[*He begins to construct the scarecrow, while Goody Rickby, assisting, brings the constructive parts from various nooks and corners.*]

We are all pretty artists, to be sure, Bessie. Phidias, he sculptures the gods; Raphael, he paints the angels; the Lord God, he creates Adam; and Dickon—fetch me the poker— aha! Dickon! What doth Dickon? He nullifies 'em all; he endows the Scarecrow!—A poker: here's his conscience. There's two fine legs to walk on,—imagination and conscience. Yonder flails now! The ideal—the *beau idéal*, dame—that's what we artists seek. The apotheosis of scarecrows! And pray, what's a scarecrow? Why, the antithesis of Adam.—"Let there be candles!" quoth the Lord God, sitting in the dark. "Let there be candle-extinguishers," saith Dickon. "I am made in the image of my maker," quoth Adam. "Look at yourself in the glass," saith Goodman Scarecrow. [*Taking two implements from Goody Rickby.*] Fine! fine! here are flails—one for wit, t'other for satire. *Sapristi!* I with two such arms, my lad, how thou wilt work thy way in the world!

GOODY RICKBY You talk as if you were making a real mortal, Dickon.

DICKON To fool a crow, Goody, I must fashion a crittur that will first deceive a man.

GOODY RICKBY He'll scarce do that without a head. [*Pointing to the loft.*] What think ye of yonder Jack-o'-lantern? 'Twas made last Hallowe'en.

DICKON Rare, my Psyche! We shall collaborate. Here!

[*Running up the ladder, he tosses down a yellow hollowed pumpkin to Goody Rickby, who catches it. Then rummaging forth an armful of cornstalks, ears, tassels, dried squashes, gourds, beets, etc., he descends and throws them in a heap on the floor.*]

Whist! the anatomy.

GOODY RICKBY [*Placing the pumpkin on the shoulders.*] Look!

DICKON *O Johannes Baptista!* What wouldst thou have given for such a head! I helped Salome to cut his off, dame, and it looked not half so appetizing on her charger. Tut! Copernicus wore once such a pumpkin, but it is rotten. Look at his golden smile! Hail, Phœbus Apollo!

GOODY RICKBY 'Tis the finest scarecrow in town.

DICKON Nay, poor soul, 'tis but a skeleton yet. He must have a man's heart in him. [*Picking a big red beet from among the cornstalks, he places it under the left side of the ribs.*] Hush! Dost thou hear it *beat*?

GOODY RICKBY Thou merry rogue!

DICKON Now for the lungs of him. [*Snatching a small pair of bellows from a peg on the wall.*] That's for eloquence! He'll preach the black knaves a sermon on theft. And now—

[*Here, with Goody Rickby's help, he stuffs the framework with the gourds, corn, etc., from the loft, weaving the husks about the legs and arms.*]

here goes for digestion and inherited instincts! More corn, Goody. Now he'll fight for his own flesh and blood!

GOODY RICKBY [*Laughing.*] Dickon, I am proud of thee.

DICKON Wait till you see his peruke. [*Seizing a feather duster made of crow's feathers.*] *Voici!* Scalps of the enemy!

[*Pulling them apart, he arranges the feathers on the pumpkin, like a gentleman's wig.*]

A rare conqueror!

GOODY RICKBY Oh, you beauty!

DICKON And now a bit of comfort for dark days and stormy nights.

[*Taking a piece of corn-cob with the kernels on it, Dickon makes a pipe, which he puts into the scarecrow's mouth.*]

So! There, Goody! I tell thee, with yonder brand-new coat and breeches of mine— those there in my cupboard!—we'll make him a lad to be proud of.

[*Taking the clothes, which Goody Rickby brings—a pair of fine scarlet breeches and a gold-embroidered coat with ruffles of lace—he puts them upon the scarecrow. Then, eying it like a connoisseur, makes a few finishing touches.*]

Why, dame, he'll be a son to thee.

GOODY RICKBY A son? Ay, if I had but a son!

DICKON Why, here you have him. [*To the scarecrow.*] Thou wilt scare the crows off thy mother's corn-field— won't my pretty? And send 'em all over t'other side the wall—to her dear neighbour's, the Justice Gilead Merton's.

GOODY RICKBY Justice Merton! Nay, if they'd only peck his eyes out, instead of his corn.

DICKON [*Grinning.*] Yet the Justice was a dear friend of "Blacksmith Bess."

GOODY RICKBY Ay, "Blacksmith Bess!" If I hadn't had a good stout arm when he cast me off with the babe, I might have starved for all his worship cared.

DICKON True, Bessie; 'twas a scurvy trick he played on thee—and on me, that took such pains to bring you together—to steal a young maid's heart—

GOODY RICKBY And then toss it away like a bad penny to the gutter! And the child—to die! [*Lifting her hammer in rage.*] Ha! if I could get the worshipful Justice Gilead into my power again— [*Drops the hammer sullenly on the anvil.*] But no! I shall beat my life away on this anvil, whilst my justice clinks his gold, and drinks his port to a fat old age. Justice! Ha—justice of God!

DICKON Whist, dame! Talk of angels and hear the rustle of their relatives.

GOODY RICKBY [*Turning, watches outside a girl's figure approaching.*] His niece— Rachel Merton! What can she want so early? Nay, I mind me; 'tis the mirror. She's a maid after our own hearts, boy,—no Sabbath-go-to-meeting airs about *her*! She hath read the books of the *magi* from cover to cover, and paid me good guineas for 'em, though her uncle knows naught on't. Besides, she's in love, Dickon.

DICKON [*Indicating the scarecrow.*] Ah? With *him*? Is it a rendezvous?

GOODY RICKBY [*With a laugh.*] Pff! Begone!

DICKON [*Shakes his finger at the scarecrow.*] Thou naughty rogue!

[*Then, still smiling slyly, with his head placed confidentially next to the scarecrow's ear, as if whispering, and with his hand pointing to the maiden outside, Dickon fades away into air. RACHEL enters, nervous and hesitant. Goody Rickby makes her a courtesy, which she acknowledges by a nod, half absent-minded.*]

GOODY RICKBY Mistress Rachel Merton—so early! I hope your uncle, our worshipful Justice, is not ill?

RACHEL No, my uncle is quite well. The early morning suits me best for a walk. You are—quite alone?

GOODY RICKBY Quite alone, mistress.   [*Bitterly.*]   Oh, folks don't call on Goody Rickby—except on business.

RACHEL [*Absently, looking round in the dim shop.*] Yes—you must be busy. Is it—is it here?

GOODY RICKBY You mean the—

RACHEL [*Starting back, with a cry.*] Ah! who's that?

GOODY RICKBY [*Chuckling.*] Fear not, mistress; 'tis nothing but a scarecrow. I'm going to put him in my corn-field yonder. The crows are so pesky this year.

RACHEL [*Draws her skirts away with a shiver.*] How loathsome!

GOODY RICKBY [*Vastly pleased.*] He'll do!

RACHEL Ah, here!—This is *the* mirror?

GOODY RICKBY Yea, mistress, and a wonderful glass it is, as I told you. I wouldn't sell it to most comers, but seeing how you and Master Talbot—

RACHEL Yes; that will do.

GOODY RICKBY You see, if the town folks guessed what it was, well—You've heard tell of the gibbets on Salem hill? There's not many in New England like you, Mistress Rachel. You know enough to approve some miracles—outside the Scriptures.

RACHEL You are quite sure the glass will do all you say? It—never fails?

GOODY RICKBY Ay, now, mistress, how could it? 'Tis the glass of truth— [*insinuatingly*] the glass of true lovers. It shows folks just as they are; no shams, no varnish. If your sweetheart be false, the glass will reveal it. If a wolf should dress himself in a white sheep's wool, this glass would reflect the black beast inside it.

RACHEL But what of the sins of the soul, Goody? Vanity, hypocrisy, and—and inconstancy? Will it surely reveal them?

GOODY RICKBY I have told you, my young lady. If it doth not as I say, bring it back and get your money again. Trust me, sweeting, 'tis your only mouse-trap for a man. Why, an old dame hath eyes in her heart yet. If your lover be false, this glass shall pluck his fine feathers!

RACHEL [*With aloofness.*] 'Tis no question of that. I wish the glass to—to amuse me.

GOODY RICKBY [*Laughing.*] Why, then, it shall amuse you. Try it on some of your neighbours.

RACHEL You ask a large price for it.

GOODY RICKBY [*Shrugs.*] I run risks. Besides, where will you get another?

RACHEL That is true. Here, I will buy it. That is the sum you mentioned, I believe?

[*She hands a purse to Goody Rickby who opens it and counts over some coins.*]

GOODY RICKBY Let see; let see.

RACHEL Well?

GOODY RICKBY Good: 'tis good. Folks call me a witch, mistress. Well—harkee—a witch's word is as good as a justice's gold. The glass is yours—with my blessing.

RACHEL Spare yourself that, dame. But the glass: how am I to get it? How will you send it to me—quietly?

GOODY RICKBY Trust me for that. I've a willing lad that helps me with such errands; a neighbour o' mine. [*Calls.*] Ebenezer!

RACHEL [*Startled.*] What! is he here?

GOODY RICKBY In the hay-loft. The boy's an orphan; he sleeps there o' times. Ebenezer!

[*A raw, dishevelled country boy appears in the loft, slides down the ladder, and shuffles up sleepily.*]

THE BOY Evenin'.

RACHEL [*Drawing Goody Rickby aside.*] You understand; I desire no comment about this purchase.

GOODY RICKBY Nor I, mistress, be sure.

RACHEL Is he—?

GOODY RICKBY [*Tapping her forehead significantly.*] Trust his wits who hath no wit; he's mum.

RACHEL Oh!

THE BOY [*Gaping.*] Job?

GOODY RICKBY Yea, rumple-head! His job this morning is to bear yonder glass to the house of Justice Merton—the big one on the hill; to the side door. Mind, no gabbing. Doth he catch?

THE BOY [*Nodding and grinning.*] 'E swallows.

RACHEL But is the boy strong enough?

GOODY RICKBY Him? [*Pointing to the anvil.*] Ebenezer!

[*The boy spits on his palms, takes hold of the anvil, lifts it, drops it again, sits on it, and grins at the door, just as Richard Talbot appears there, from outside.*]

RACHEL Gracious!

GOODY RICKBY Trust him. He'll carry the glass for you.

RACHEL I will return home at once, then. Let him go quietly to the side door, and wait for me. Good morning. [*Turning, she confronts Richard.*]

RICHARD Good morning.

RACHEL Richard!—Squire Talbot, you—you are abroad early.

RICHARD As early as Mistress Rachel. Is it pardonable? I caught sight of you walking in this direction, so I thought it wise to follow, lest— [*Looks hard at Goody Rickby.*]

RACHEL Very kind. Thanks. I've done my errand. Well; we can return together. [*To Goody Rickby.*] You will make sure that I receive the—the article.

GOODY RICKBY Trust me, mistress. [*Courtesying.*] Squire Talbot! the honour, sir!

RICHARD [*Bluntly, looking from one to the other.*] What article?

[*Rachel ignores the question and starts to pass out. Richard frowns at Goody Rickby, who stammers.*]

GOODY RICKBY Begging your pardon, sir?

RICHARD What article? I said. [*After a short, embarrassed pause: more sternly.*] Well?

GOODY RICKBY Oh, the article! Yonder old glass, to be sure, sir. A quaint piece, your honour.

RICHARD Rachel, you haven't come here at sunrise to buy—that thing?

RACHEL Verily, "that thing" and at sunrise. A pretty time for a pretty purchase. Are you coming?

RICHARD [*In a low voice.*] More witchcraft nonsense? Do you realize this is serious?

RACHEL Oh, of course. You know I am desperately mystical, so pray let us not discuss it. Good-by.

RICHARD Rachel, just a moment. If you want a mirror, you shall have the prettiest one in New England. Or I will import you one from London. Only—I beg of you—don't buy stolen goods.

GOODY RICKBY Stolen goods?

RACHEL [*Aside to Richard.*] Don't! don't!

RICHARD At least, articles under suspicion. [*To Goody Rickby.*] Can you account for this mirror—how you came by it?

GOODY RICKBY I'll show ye! I'll show ye! Stolen—ha!

RICHARD Come, old swindler, keep your mirror, and give this lady back her money.

GOODY RICKBY I'll damn ye both, I will!—Stolen!

RACHEL [*Imploringly.*] Will you come?

RICHARD Look you, old Rickby; this is not the first time. Charm all the broomsticks in town, if you like; bewitch all the tables and saucepans and mirrors you please; but gull no more money out of young girls. Mind you! We're not so enterprising in this town as at Salem; but—*it may come to it*! So look sharp! I'm not blind to what's going on here.

GOODY RICKBY Not blind, Master Puritan? Oho! You can see through all my counterfeits, can ye? So! you would scrape all the wonder out'n the world, as I've scraped all the meat out'n my punkin-head yonder! Aha! wait and see! Afore sundown, I'll send ye a nut to crack, shall make your orthodox jaws ache. Your servant, Master Deuteronomy!

RICHARD [*To Rachel, who has seized his arm.*] We'll go. [*Exeunt Richard and Rachel.*]

GOODY RICKBY [*Calls shrilly after them.*] Trot away, pretty team; toss your heads. I'll unhitch ye and take off your blinders.

THE SLOUCHING BOY [*Capering and grimacing in front of the mirror, shrieks with laughter.*] Ohoho!

GOODY RICKBY [*Returning, savagely.*] Yes, yes, my fine lover! I'll pay thee for "stolen goods"—I'll pay thee. [*Screams.*] Dickon! Stop laughing.

THE BOY O Lord! O Lord!

GOODY RICKBY What tickles thy mirth now?

THE BOY For to think as the soul of an orphan innocent, what lives in a hay-loft, should wear horns.

[*On looking into the mirror, the spectator perceives therein that the reflection of the slouching boy is the horned demon figure of Dickon, who performs the same antics in pantomime within the glass as the boy does without.*]

GOODY RICKBY Yea; 'tis a wise devil that knows his own face in the glass. But hark now! Thou must find me a rival for this cock-squire,—dost hear? A rival, that shall steal away the heart of his Mistress Rachel.

DICKON And take her to church?

GOODY RICKBY To church or to Hell. All's one.

DICKON A rival! [*Pointing at the glass.*] How would *he* serve—in there? Dear Ebenezer! Fancy the deacons in the vestry, Goody, and her uncle, the Justice, when they saw him escorting the bride to the altar, with his tail round her waist!

GOODY RICKBY Tut, tut! Think it over in earnest, and meantime take her the glass. Wait, we'd best fold it up small, so as not to attract notice on the road.

[*Dickon, who has already drawn the curtains over the glass, grasps one side of the large frame, Goody Rickby the other.*]

Now!

[*Pushing their shoulders against the two sides, the frame disappears and Dickon holds in his hand a mirror about a foot square, of the same design.*]

So! Be off! And mind, a rival for Richard!

DICKON For Richard a rival, Dear Goody Rickby Wants Dickon's connival: Lord! What can the trick be? [*To the scarecrow.*] By-by, Sonny; take care of thy mother.

[*Dickon slouches out with the glass, whistling.*]

GOODY RICKBY Mother! Yea, if only I had a son—the Justice Merton's and mine! If the brat had but lived now to remind him of those merry days, which he has forgotten. Zooks, wouldn't I put a spoke in his wheel! But no such luck for me! No such luck!

[*As she goes to the forge, the stout figure of a man appears in the doorway behind her. Under one arm he carries a large book, in the other hand a gold-headed cane. He hesitates, embarrassed.*]

THE MAN Permit me, Madam.

GOODY RICKBY [*Turning.*] Ah, him!—Justice Merton!

JUSTICE MERTON [*Removing his hat, steps over the sill, and lays his great book on the table; then with a supercilious look, he puts his hat firmly on again.*] Permit me, dame.

GOODY RICKBY You!

[*With confused, affected hauteur, the Justice shifts from foot to foot, flourishing his cane. As he speaks, Goody Rickby, with a shrewd, painful expression, draws slowly backward toward the door left, which opens into an inner room. Reaching it, she opens it part way, stands facing him, and listens.*]

JUSTICE MERTON I have had the honour—permit me—to entertain suspicions; to rise early, to follow my niece, to meet just now Squire Talbot, an excellent young gentleman of wealth, if not of fashion; to hear his remarks concerning—hem!—you, dame! to call here—permit me—to express myself and inquire—

GOODY RICKBY Concerning your waistcoat?

[*Turning quickly, she snatches an article of apparel which hangs on the inner side of the door, and holds it up.*]

JUSTICE MERTON [*Starting, crimson.*] Woman!

GOODY RICKBY You left it behind—the last time.

JUSTICE MERTON I have not the honour to remember—

GOODY RICKBY The one I embroidered?

JUSTICE MERTON 'Tis a matter—

GOODY RICKBY Of some two and twenty years. [*Stretching out the narrow width of the waistcoat.*] Will you try it on now, dearie?

JUSTICE MERTON Unconscionable! Un-un-unconscionable witch!

GOODY RICKBY Witchling—thou used to say.

JUSTICE MERTON

Pah! pah! I forget myself. Pride, permit me, goeth before a fall. As a magistrate, Rickby, I have already borne with you long! The last straw, however, breaks the camel's back.

GOODY RICKBY Poor camel!

JUSTICE MERTON You have soiled, you have smirched, the virgin reputation of my niece. You have inveigled her into notions of witchcraft; already the neighbours are beginning to talk. 'Tis a long lane which hath no turning, saith the Lord. Permit me— as a witch, thou art judged. Thou shalt hang.

A VOICE [*Behind him.*] And me too?

JUSTICE MERTON [*Turns about and stares.*] I beg pardon.

THE VOICE [*In front of him.*] Not at all.

JUSTICE MERTON Did—did somebody speak?

THE VOICE Don't you recognize my voice? *Still and small*, you know. If you will kindly let me out, we can chat.

JUSTICE MERTON [*Turning fiercely on Goody Rickby.*] These are thy sorceries. But I fear them not. The righteous man walketh with God. [*Going to the book which lies on the table.*] Satan, I ban thee! I will read from the Holy Scriptures!

[*Unclasping the Bible, he flings open the ponderous covers.—Dickon steps forth in smoke.*]

DICKON Thanks; it was stuffy in there.

JUSTICE MERTON [*Clasping his hands.*] Dickon!

DICKON [*Moving a step nearer on the table.*] Hillo, Gilly! Hillo, Bess!

JUSTICE MERTON Dickon! No! No!

DICKON Do ye mind Auld Lang Syne—the chorus that night, Gilly? [*Sings.*] Gil-ead, Gil-ead, Gil-ead Merton, He was a silly head, silly head, Certain, When he forgot to steal a bed-Curtain! *Encore*, now!

JUSTICE MERTON No, no, be merciful! I will not harm her; she shall not hang: I swear, I swear it! [*Dickon disappears.*] I swear—ah! Is he gone? Witchcraft! Witchcraft! I have witnessed it. 'Tis proved on thee, slut. I swear it: thou shalt hang. [*Exit wildly.*]

GOODY RICKBY Ay, Gilead! I shall hang *on*! Ahaha! Dickon, thou angel! Ah, Satan!

Satan! For a son now!

DICKON [*Reappearing.*] *Videlicet*, in law—a bastard. *N'est ce pas?*

GOODY RICKBY Yea, in law and in justice, I should-a had one now. Worse luck that he died.

DICKON One and twenty years ago? [*Goody Rickby nods.*] Good; he should be of age now. One and twenty—a pretty age, too, for a rival. Haha!—For arrival?—Marry, he shall arrive, then; arrive and marry and inherit his patrimony—all on his birthday! Come, to work!

GOODY RICKBY What rant is this?

DICKON Yet, Dickon, it pains me to perform such an anachronism. All this Mediævalism in Massachusetts!—These old-fashioned flames and alchemic accompaniments, when I've tried so hard to be a native American product; it jars. But *che vuole*! I'm naturally middle-aged. I haven't been really myself, let me think,—since 1492!

GOODY RICKBY What art thou mooning about?

DICKON [*Still impenetrable.*] There was my old friend in Germany, Dr. Johann Faustus; he was nigh such a bag of old rubbish when I made him over. Ain't it trite! No, you can't teach an old dog like me new tricks. Still, a scarecrow! that's decidedly local color. Come then; a Yankee masterpiece!

[*Seizing Goody Rickby by the arm, and placing her before the scarecrow, he makes a bow and wave of introduction.*]

Behold, madam, your son—illegitimate; the future affianced of Mistress Rachel Merton, the heir-elect, through matrimony, of Merton House,—Gilead Merton second; Lord Ravensbane! Your lordship—your mother.

GOODY RICKBY Dickon! Can you do it?

DICKON I can—try.

GOODY RICKBY You will create him for me?— [*Wickedly.*] and for Gilead!

DICKON I will—for a kiss.

GOODY RICKBY [*About to embrace him.*] Dickon!

DICKON [*Dodging her.*] Later. Now, the waistcoat.

GOODY RICKBY [*Handing it.*] Rare! rare! He shall go wooing in't—like his father.

DICKON [*Shifting the scarecrow's gold-trimmed coat, slips on the embroidered waistcoat and replaces the coat.*] Stand still, Jack! So, my macaroni. *Perfecto!* Stay—a walking-stick!

GOODY RICKBY [*Wrenching a spoke out of an old rickety wheel.*] Here: the spoke for Gilead. He used to take me to drive in the chaise it came out of.

DICKON [*Placing the spoke as a cane, in the scarecrow's sleeve, views him with satisfaction.*] *Sic!* There, Jacky! *Filius fit non nascitur.*—Sam Hill! My Latin is stale. "In the beginning, was the—gourd!" Of these thy modest ingredients may thy spirit smack!

[*Making various mystic passes with his hands, Dickon intones, now deep and solemn, now with fanciful shrill rapidity, this incantation:*]

Flail, flip; Broom, sweep; *Sic itur!* Cornstalk And turnip, talk! Turn crittur!

Pulse, beet; Gourd, eat; *Ave* Hellas! Poker and punkin, Stir the old junk in: Breathe, bellows!

Corn-cob, And crow's feather, End the job: Jumble the rest o' the rubbish together; Dovetail and tune 'em. *E pluribus unum!*

[*The scarecrow remains stock still.*]

The devil! Have I lost the hang of it? Ah! Hullo! He's dropped his pipe. What's a dandy without his 'baccy! [*Restoring the corn-cob pipe to the scarecrow's mouth.*] 'Tis the life and breath of him. So; hand me yon hazel switch, Goody. [*Waving it.*] Presto! Brighten, coal, I' the dusk between us! Whiten, soul! *Propinquit Venus!*

[*A whiff of smoke puffs from the scarecrow's pipe.*] *Sic! Sic! Jacobus!* [*Another whiff.*] Bravo! [*The whiffs grow more rapid and the thing trembles.*]

GOODY RICKBY Puff! puff, manny, for thy life!

DICKON *Fiat, fœtus!*—Huzza! *Noch einmal!* Go it!

[*Clouds of smoke issue from the pipe, half fill the shop, and envelop the creature, who staggers.*][1]

GOODY RICKBY See! See his eyes!

DICKON [*Beckoning with one finger.*] *Veni, fili! Veni!* Take 'ee first step, *bambino!*— Toddle!

[*The Scarecrow makes a stiff lurch forward and falls sidewise against the anvil, propped half-reclining against which he leans rigid, emitting fainter puffs of smoke in gasps.*]

GOODY RICKBY [*Screams.*] Have a care! He's fallen.

DICKON Well done, Punkin Jack! Thou shalt be knighted for that! [*Striking him on the shoulder with the hazel rod.*] Rise, Lord Ravensbane! [*The Scarecrow totters to his*

1   Here the living actor, through a trap, concealed by the smoke, will substitute himself for the elegantly clad effigy. His make-up, of course, will approximate to the latter, but the grotesque contours of his expression gradually, throughout the remainder of the act, become refined and sublimated till, at the finale, they are of a lordly and distinguished caste.

feet, and makes a forlorn rectilinear salutation.]

GOODY RICKBY Look! He bows.—He flaps his flails at thee. He smiles like a tik-doo-loo-roo!

DICKON [*With a profound reverence, backing away.*] Will his lordship deign to follow his tutor? [*With hitches and jerks, the Scarecrow follows Dickon.*]

GOODY RICKBY O Lord! Lord! the style o' the broomstick!

DICKON [*Holding ready a high-backed chair.*] Will his lordship be seated and rest himself?

[*Awkwardly the Scarecrow half falls into the chair; his head sinks sideways, and his pipe falls out. Dickon snatches it up instantly and restores it to his mouth.*]

Puff! Puff, *puer*; 'tis thy life. [*The Scarecrow puffs again.*] Is his lordship's tobacco refreshing?

GOODY RICKBY Look now! The red colour in his cheeks. The beet-juice is pumping, oho!

DICKON [*Offering his arm.*] Your lordship will deign to receive an audience? [*The Scarecrow takes his arm and rises.*] The Marchioness of Rickby, your lady mother, entreats leave to present herself.

GOODY RICKBY [*Courtesying low.*] My son!

DICKON [*Holding the pipe, and waving the hazel rod.*] *Dicite!* Speak!

[*The Scarecrow, blowing out his last mouthful of smoke, opens his mouth, gasps, gurgles, and is silent.*]

In principio erat verbum! Accost thy mother!

[*The Scarecrow, clutching at his side in a struggle for coherence, fixes a pathetic look of pain on Goody Rickby.*]

THE SCARECROW Mother!

GOODY RICKBY [*With a scream of hysterical laughter, seizes both Dickon's hands and dances him about the forge.*] O Beelzebub! I shall die!

DICKON Thou hast thy son. [*Dickon whispers in the Scarecrow's ear, shakes his finger, and exit.*]

GOODY RICKBY He called me "mother." Again, boy, again.

THE SCARECROW From the bottom of my heart—mother.

GOODY RICKBY "The bottom of his heart"—Nay, thou killest me.

THE SCARECROW Permit me, madam!

GOODY RICKBY Gilead! Gilead himself! Waistcoat, "permit me," and all: thy father over again, I tell thee.

THE SCARECROW [*With a slight stammer.*] It gives me—I assure you—lady—the deepest happiness.

GOODY RICKBY Just so the old hypocrite spoke when I said I'd have him. But thou hast a sweeter deference, my son.

[*Re-enter Dickon; he is dressed all in black, save for a white stock,—a suit of plain elegance.*]

DICKON Now, my lord, your tutor is ready.

THE SCARECROW [*To Goody Rickby.*] I have the honour—permit me—to wish you—good morning.

[*Bows and takes a step after Dickon, who, taking a three-cornered cocked hat from a peg, goes toward the door.*]

GOODY RICKBY Whoa! Whoa, Jack! Whither away?

DICKON [*Presenting the hat.*] Deign to reply, sir.

THE SCARECROW I go—with my tutor—Master Dickonson—to pay my respects— to his worship—the Justice—Merton—to solicit—the hand—of his daughter—the fair Mistress—Rachel. [*With another bow.*] Permit me.

GOODY RICKBY Permit ye? God speed ye! Thou must teach him his tricks, Dickon.

DICKON Trust me, Goody. Between here and Justice Merton's, I will play the mother-hen, and I promise thee, our bantling shall be as stuffed with compliments as a callow chick with caterpillars.

[*As he throws open the big doors, the cawing of crows is heard again.*]

Hark! your lordship's retainers acclaim you on your birthday. They bid you welcome to your majority. Listen! "Long live Lord Ravensbane! Caw!"

GOODY RICKBY Look! Count 'em, Dickon. One for sorrow, Two for mirth, Three for a wedding, Four for a birth— Four on 'em! So! Good luck on thy birthday! And see! There's three on 'em flying into the Justice's field. —Flight o' the crows Tells how the wind blows!— A wedding! Get ye gone. Wed the girl, and sting the Justice. Bless ye, my son!

THE SCARECROW [*With a profound reverence.*]

Mother—believe me—to be—your ladyship's— most devoted—and obedient—son.

DICKON [*Prompting him aloud.*] Ravensbane.

THE SCARECROW [*Donning his hat, lifts his head in hauteur, shakes his lace ruffle over his hand, turns his shoulder, nods slightly, and speaks for the first time with complete mastery of his voice.*] Hm! Ravensbane! [*With one hand in the arm of Dickon, the other twirling his cane (the converted chaise-spoke), wreathed in halos of smoke from his pipe, the fantastical figure hitches elegantly forth into the daylight, amid louder acclamations of the crows.*]

ACT II

The same morning. Justice Merton's parlour, furnished and designed in the style of the early colonial period. On the right wall, hangs a portrait of the Justice as a young man; on the left wall, an old-fashioned looking-glass. At the right of the room stands the Glass of Truth, draped—as in the blacksmith shop—with the strange, embroidered curtain.

In front of it are discovered RACHEL *and* RICHARD; *Rachel is about to draw the curtain.*

RACHEL Now! Are you willing?

RICHARD So you suspect me of dark, villainous practices?

RACHEL No, no, foolish Dick.

RICHARD Still, I am to be tested; is that it?

RACHEL That's it.

RICHARD As your true lover.

RACHEL Well, yes.

RICHARD Why, of course, then, I consent. A true lover always consents to the follies of his lady-love.

RACHEL Thank you, Dick; I trust the glass will sustain your character. Now; when I draw the curtain—

RICHARD [*Staying her hand.*] What if I be false?

RACHEL Then, sir, the glass will reflect you as the subtle fox that you are.

RICHARD And you—as the goose?

RACHEL Very likely. Ah! but, Richard dear, we mustn't laugh. It may prove very serious. You do not guess—you do not dream all the mysteries—

RICHARD [*Shaking his head, with a grave smile.*] You pluck at too many mysteries; sometime they may burn your fingers. Remember our first mother Eve!

RACHEL But this is the glass of truth; and Goody Rickby told me—

RICHARD Rickby, forsooth!

RACHEL Nay, come; let's have it over.

[*She draws the curtain, covers her eyes, steps back by Richard's side, looks at the glass, and gives a joyous cry.*]

Ah! there you are, dear! There we are, both of us—just as we have always seemed to each other, true. 'Tis proved. Isn't it wonderful?

RICHARD Miraculous! That a mirror bought in a blacksmith shop, before sunrise, for twenty pounds, should prove to be actually—a mirror!

RACHEL Richard, I'm so happy.

[*Enter* JUSTICE MERTON *and* MISTRESS MERTON.]

RICHARD [*Embracing her.*] Happy, art thou, sweet goose? Why, then, God bless Goody Rickby.

JUSTICE MERTON Strange words from you, Squire Talbot.

[*Rachel and Richard part quickly; Rachel draws the curtain over the mirror; Richard stands stiffly.*]

RICHARD Justice Merton! Why, sir, the old witch is more innocent, perhaps, than I represented her.

JUSTICE MERTON A witch, believe me, is never innocent. [*Taking their hands, he brings them together and kisses Rachel on the forehead.*] Permit me, young lovers. I was once young myself, young and amorous.

MISTRESS MERTON [*In a low voice.*] Verily!

JUSTICE MERTON My fair niece, my worthy young man, beware of witchcraft.

MISTRESS MERTON And Goody Rickby, too, brother?

JUSTICE MERTON That woman shall answer for her deeds. She is proscribed.

RACHEL Proscribed? What is that?

MISTRESS MERTON [*Examining the mirror.*] What is this?

JUSTICE MERTON She shall hang.

RACHEL Uncle, no! Not merely because of my purchase this morning.

JUSTICE MERTON Your purchase?

MISTRESS MERTON [*Pointing to the mirror.*] That, I suppose.

JUSTICE MERTON What! you purchased that mirror of her? You brought it here?

RACHEL No, the boy brought it; I found it here when I returned.

JUSTICE MERTON What! From her! You purchased it? From her shop? From her infamous den, into my parlour! [*To Mistress Merton.*] Call the servant. [*Himself calling.*] Micah! This instant, this instant—away with it! Micah!

RACHEL Uncle Gilead, I bought—

JUSTICE MERTON Micah, I say! Where is the man?

RACHEL Listen, Uncle. I bought it with my own money.

JUSTICE MERTON Thine own money! Wilt have the neighbours gossip? Wilt have me, thyself, my house, suspected of complicity with witches? [*Enter* MICAH.] Micah, take this away.

MICAH Yes, sir; but, sir—

JUSTICE MERTON Out of my house!

MICAH There be visitors.

JUSTICE MERTON Away with—

MISTRESS MERTON [*Touching his arm.*] Gilead!

MICAH Visitors, sir; gentry.

JUSTICE MERTON Ah!

MICAH Shall I show them in, sir?

JUSTICE MERTON Visitors! In the morning? Who are they?

MICAH Strangers, sir. I should judge they be very high gentry; lords, sir.

ALL Lords!

MICAH At least, one on 'em, sir. The other—the dark gentleman—told me they left their horses at the inn, sir.

MISTRESS MERTON Hark! [*The faces of all wear suddenly a startled expression.*] Where is that unearthly sound?

JUSTICE MERTON [*Listening.*] Is it in the cellar?

MICAH 'Tis just the dog howling, madam. When he spied the gentry he turned tail and run below.

MISTRESS MERTON Oh, the dog!

JUSTICE MERTON Show the gentlemen here, Micah. Don't keep them waiting. [*Exit* MICAH.] A lord! [*To Rachel.*] We shall talk of this matter later.—A lord! [*Turning to the small glass on the wall, he arranges his peruke and attire.*]

RACHEL [*To Richard.*] What a fortunate interruption! But, dear Dick! I wish we needn't meet these strangers now.

RICHARD Would you really rather we were alone together? [*They chat aside, absorbed in each other.*]

JUSTICE MERTON Think of it, Cynthia, a lord!

MISTRESS MERTON [*Dusting the furniture hastily with her handkerchief.*] And such dust!

RACHEL [*To Richard.*] You know, dear, we need only be introduced, and then we can steal away together. [*Re-enter* MICAH.]

MICAH [*Announcing.*] Lord Ravensbane: Marquis of Oxford, Baron of Wittenberg, Elector of Worms, and Count of Cordova; Master Dickonson.

[*Enter* RAVENSBANE *and* DICKON.]

JUSTICE MERTON Gentlemen, permit me, you are excessively welcome. I am deeply gratified to meet—

DICKON Lord Ravensbane, of the Rookeries, Somersetshire.

JUSTICE MERTON Lord Ravensbane—his lordship's most truly honoured.

RAVENSBANE Truly honoured.

JUSTICE MERTON [*Turning to Dickon.*] His lordship's—?

DICKON Tutor.

JUSTICE MERTON [*Checking his effusiveness.*] Ah, so!

DICKON Justice Merton, I believe.

JUSTICE MERTON Of Merton House.—May I present—permit me, your lordship— my sister, Mistress Merton.

RAVENSBANE Mistress Merton.

JUSTICE MERTON And my—and my— [*Under his breath.*] Rachel! [*Rachel remains with a bored expression behind Richard.*] —my young neighbour, Squire Talbot, Squire Richard Talbot of—of—

RICHARD Of nowhere, sir.

RAVENSBANE [*Nods.*] Nowhere.

JUSTICE MERTON And permit me, Lord Ravensbane, my niece—Mistress Rachel Merton.

RAVENSBANE [*Bows low.*] Mistress Rachel Merton.

RACHEL [*Courtesies.*] Lord Ravensbane.

[*As they raise their heads, their eyes meet and are fascinated. Dickon just then takes Ravensbane's pipe and fills it.*]

RAVENSBANE Mistress Rachel!

RACHEL Your lordship! [*Dickon returns the pipe.*]

MISTRESS MERTON A pipe! Gilead!—in the parlour! [*Justice Merton frowns silence.*]

JUSTICE MERTON Your lordship—ahem!—has just arrived in town?

DICKON From London, via New Amsterdam.

RICHARD [*Aside.*] Is he staring at *you*? Are you ill, Rachel?

RACHEL [*Indifferently.*] What?

JUSTICE MERTON Lord Ravensbane honours my humble roof.

DICKON [*Touches Ravensbane's arm.*] Your lordship—"roof."

RAVENSBANE [*Starting, turns to Merton.*] Nay, sir, the roof of my father's oldest friend bestows generous hospitality upon his only son.

JUSTICE MERTON Only son—ah, yes! Your father—

RAVENSBANE My father, I trust, sir, has never forgotten the intimate companionship, the touching devotion, the unceasing solicitude for his happiness which you, sir, manifested to him in the days of his youth.

JUSTICE MERTON Really, your lordship, the—the slight favours which—hem! some years ago, I was privileged to show your illustrious father—

RAVENSBANE Permit me!—Because, however, of his present infirmities—for I regret to say that my father is suffering a temporary aberration of mind—

JUSTICE MERTON You distress me!

RAVENSBANE My lady mother has charged me with a double mission here in New England. On my quitting my home, sir, to explore the wideness and the mystery of this world, my mother bade me be sure to call upon his worship, the Justice Merton; and deliver to him, first, my father's remembrances; and secondly, my mother's epistle.

DICKON [*Handing to Justice Merton a sealed document.*] Her ladyship's letter, sir.

JUSTICE MERTON [*Examining the seal with awe, speaks aside to Mistress Merton.*] Cynthia!—a crested seal!

DICKON His lordship's crest, sir: rooks rampant.

JUSTICE MERTON [*Embarrassed, breaks the seal.*] Permit me.

RACHEL [*Looking at Ravensbane.*] Have you noticed his bearing, Richard: what personal distinction! what inbred nobility! Every inch a true lord!

RICHARD He may be a lord, my dear, but he walks like a broomstick.

RACHEL How dare you! [*Turns abruptly away; as she does so, a fold of her gown catches in a chair.*]

DICKON [*To Justice Merton.*] A word, sir.

JUSTICE MERTON [*Glancing up from the letter.*] I am astonished—overpowered!

RAVENSBANE Mistress Rachel—permit me. [*Stooping, he extricates the fold of her gown.*]

RACHEL Oh, thank you. [*They go aside together.*]

RICHARD [*To Mistress Merton.*] So Lord Ravensbane and his family are old friends of yours?

MISTRESS MERTON [*Monosyllabically.*] I never heard the name before, Richard.

RICHARD Why! but I thought that your brother, the Justice—

MISTRESS MERTON The Justice is reticent.

RICHARD Ah!

MISTRESS MERTON Especially concerning his youth.

RICHARD Ah!

RAVENSBANE [*To Rachel, taking her hand after a whisper from Dickon.*] Believe me, sweet lady, it will give me the deepest pleasure.

RACHEL Can you really tell fortunes?

RAVENSBANE More than that; I can bestow them.

JUSTICE MERTON [*To Dickon.*] But is her ladyship really serious? An offer of marriage!

DICKON Pray read it again, sir.

JUSTICE MERTON [*Reads.*] "To the Worshipful, the Justice Gilead Merton, "Merton House. "My Honourable Friend and Benefactor: "With these brief lines I commend to you our son"—*our* son!

DICKON She speaks likewise for his young lordship's father, sir.

JUSTICE MERTON Ah! of course. [*Reads.*] "In a strange land, I intrust him to you as to a father." Honoured, believe me! "I have only to add my earnest hope that the natural gifts, graces, and inherited fortune"—ah—!

DICKON Twenty thousand pounds—on his father's demise.

JUSTICE MERTON Ah!—"fortune of this young scion of nobility will so propitiate the heart of your niece, Mistress Rachel Merton, as to cause her to accept his proffered hand in matrimony;" —but—but—but Squire Talbot is betrothed to—well, well, we shall see;—"in matrimony, and thus cement the early bonds of interest and affection between your honoured self and his lordship's father; not to mention, dear sir, your worship's ever grateful and obedient admirer, "ELIZABETH, "Marchioness of R."

Of R.! of R.! Will you believe me, my dear sir, so long is it since my travels in England—I visited at so many—hem! noble estates—permit me, it is so awkward, but—

DICKON [*With his peculiar intonation of Act I.*] Not at all.

JUSTICE MERTON [*Starting.*] I—I confess, sir, my youthful memory fails me. Will you be so very obliging; this—this Marchioness of R.—?

DICKON [*Enjoying his discomfiture.*] Yes?

JUSTICE MERTON The R, I presume, stands for—

DICKON Rickby.

RAVENSBANE [*Calls.*] Dickon, my pipe! [*Dickon glides away to fill Ravensbane's pipe.*]

JUSTICE MERTON [*Stands bewildered and horror-struck.*] Great God!—Thou inexorable Judge!

RICHARD [*To Mistress Merton, scowling at Ravensbane and Rachel.*] Are these court manners, in London?

MISTRESS MERTON Don't ask *me*, Richard.

RAVENSBANE [*Dejectedly to Rachel, as Dickon is refilling his pipe.*] Alas! Mistress Rachel is cruel.

RACHEL I?—cruel, your lordship?

RAVENSBANE Your own white hand has written it. [*Lifting her palm.*] See, these lines: Rejection! you will reject one who loves you dearly.

RACHEL Fie, your lordship! Be not cast down at fortune-telling. Let me tell yours, may I?

RAVENSBANE [*Rapturously holding his palm for her to examine.*] Ah! Permit me.

JUSTICE MERTON [*Murmurs, in terrible agitation.*] Dickon! Can it be Dickon?

RACHEL Why, Lord Ravensbane, your pulse. Really, if I am cruel, you are quite heartless. I declare I can't feel your heart beat at all.

RAVENSBANE Ah! mistress, that is because I have just lost it.

RACHEL [*Archly.*] Where?

RAVENSBANE [*Faintly.*] Dickon, my pipe!

RACHEL Alas! my lord, are you ill?

DICKON [*Restoring the lighted pipe to Ravensbane, speaks aside.*] Pardon me, sweet young lady, I must confide to you that his lordship's heart is peculiarly responsive to his emotions. When he feels very ardently, it quite stops. Hence the use of his pipe.

RACHEL Oh! Is smoking, then, necessary for his heart?

DICKON Absolutely—to equilibrate the valvular palpitations. Without his pipe—should his lordship experience, for instance, the emotion of love—he might die.

RACHEL You alarm me!

DICKON But this is for you only, Mistress Rachel. We may confide in you?

RACHEL Oh, utterly, sir.

DICKON His lordship, you know, is so sensitive.

RAVENSBANE [*To Rachel.*] You have given it back to me. Why did not you keep it?

RACHEL What, my lord?

RAVENSBANE My heart.

JUSTICE MERTON [*To Dickon.*] Permit me, one moment; I did not catch your name.

DICKON My name? Dickonson.

JUSTICE MERTON [*With a gasp of relief.*] Ah, Dickonson! Thank you. I mistook the word.

DICKON A compound, your worship. [*With a malignant smile.*] Dickon- [*Then jerking his thumb over his shoulder at Ravensbane.*] son! [*Bowing.*] Both at your service.

JUSTICE MERTON If—if you can show pity—speak low.

DICKON As hell, your worship?

JUSTICE MERTON Is he—he there?

DICKON Bessie's brat; yes; it didn't die, after all, poor suckling! Dickon weaned it. Saved it for balm of Gilead. Raised it for joyful home-coming. Prodigal's return! Twenty-first birthday! Happy son! Happy father!

JUSTICE MERTON My—son!

DICKON Felicitations!

JUSTICE MERTON I will not believe it.

DICKON Truth is hard fare.

JUSTICE MERTON [*Faintly.*] What—what do you want?

DICKON Only the happiness of your dear ones. [*Indicating Rachel and Ravensbane.*] The union of these young hearts and hands.

JUSTICE MERTON What! he will dare—an illegitimate—

DICKON Fie, fie, Gilly! Why, the brat is a lord now.

JUSTICE MERTON Oh, the disgrace! Spare me that, Dickon.

RICHARD [*In a low voice to Rachel, who is talking in a fascinated manner to Ravensbane.*] Are you mad?

RACHEL [*Indifferently.*] What is the matter? [*Laughing, to Ravensbane.*] Oh, your lordship is too witty!

JUSTICE MERTON [*To Dickon.*] After all, I was young then.

DICKON Quite so.

JUSTICE MERTON And she is innocent; she is already betrothed.

DICKON Twiddle-twaddle! Look at her eyes now! [*Rachel is still telling Ravensbane's fortune; and they are manifestly absorbed in each other.*] 'Tis a brilliant match; besides, her ladyship's heart is set upon it.

JUSTICE MERTON Her ladyship—?

DICKON The Marchioness of Rickby.

JUSTICE MERTON [*Glowering.*] I had forgotten.

DICKON Her ladyship has never forgotten. So, you see, your worship's alternatives are most simple. Alternative one: advance his lordship's suit with your niece as speedily as possible, and save all scandal. Alternative two: impede his lordship's suit, and—

JUSTICE MERTON Don't, Dickon! don't reveal the truth; not disgrace now!

DICKON Good; we are agreed, then?

JUSTICE MERTON I have no choice.

DICKON [*Cheerfully.*] Why, true; we ignored that, didn't we?

MISTRESS MERTON [*Approaching.*] This young lord—Why, Gilead, are you ill?

JUSTICE MERTON [*With a great effort, commands himself.*] Not in the least.

MISTRESS MERTON Rachel's deportment, my dear brother—

RACHEL I am really at a loss. Your lordship's hand is so very peculiar.

RAVENSBANE Ah! Peculiar.

RACHEL This, now, is the line of life.

RAVENSBANE Of life, yes?

RACHEL But it begins so abruptly, and see! it breaks off and ends nowhere. And just so here with this line—the line of—of love.

RAVENSBANE Of love. So; it breaks?

RACHEL Yes.

RAVENSBANE Ah, then, that must be the *heart* line.

RACHEL I am afraid your lordship is very fickle.

MISTRESS MERTON [*Horrified.*] I tell you, Gilead, they are fortune-telling!

JUSTICE MERTON Tush! Tush!

MISTRESS MERTON Tush? "*Tush*" to *me*? Tush!

[*Richard, who has been stifling his feelings at Rachel's rebuff, and has stood fidgeting at a civil distance from her, now walks up to Justice Merton.*]

RICHARD Intolerable! Do you approve of *this*, sir? Are Lord Ravensbane's credentials satisfactory?

JUSTICE MERTON Eminently, eminently.

RICHARD Ah! So her ladyship's letter is—

JUSTICE MERTON Charming; charming.

RICHARD To be sure; old friends, when they are lords, it makes such a difference.

DICKON True friends—old friends; New friends—cold friends. *N'est ce pas*, your worship?

JUSTICE MERTON Indeed, Master Dickonson; indeed! [*To Richard, as Dickon goes toward Ravensbane and Rachel.*] What happiness to encounter the manners of the nobility!

RICHARD If you approve them, sir, it is sufficient. This is your house. [*He turns away.*]

JUSTICE MERTON Your lordship will, I trust, make my house your home.

RAVENSBANE My home, sir.

RACHEL [*To Dickon, who has spoken to her.*] Really? [*To Justice Merton.*] Why, uncle, what is this Master Dickonson tells us?

JUSTICE MERTON What! What! he has revealed—

RACHEL Yes, indeed. Why did you never tell us?

JUSTICE MERTON Rachel! Rachel!

MISTRESS MERTON You are moved, brother.

RACHEL [*Laughingly to Ravensbane.*] My uncle is doubtless astonished to find you so grown.

RAVENSBANE [*Laughingly to Justice Merton.*] I am doubtless astonished, sir, to be so grown.

JUSTICE MERTON [*To Dickon.*] You have—

DICKON Remarked, sir, that your worship had often dandled his lordship—as an infant.

JUSTICE MERTON [*Smiling lugubriously.*] Quite so—as an infant merely.

RACHEL How interesting! Then you must have seen his lordship's home in England.

JUSTICE MERTON As you say.

RACHEL [*To Ravensbane.*] Do describe it to us. We are so isolated here from the grand world. Do you know, I always imagine England to be an enchanted isle, like one of the old Hesperides, teeming with fruits of solid gold.

RAVENSBANE Ah, yes! my mother raises them.

RACHEL Fruits of gold?

RAVENSBANE Round like the rising sun. She calls them—ah! punkins.

MISTRESS MERTON "Punkins!"

JUSTICE MERTON [*Aside, grinding his teeth.*] Scoundrel! Scoundrel!

RACHEL [*Laughing.*] Your lordship pokes fun at us.

DICKON His lordship is an artist in words, mistress. I have noticed that in whatever country he is travelling, he tinges his vocabulary with the local idiom. His lordship means, of course, not pumpkins, but pomegranates.

RACHEL We forgive him. But, your lordship, please be serious and describe to us your hall.

RAVENSBANE Quite serious: the hall. Yes, yes; in the middle burns a great fire—on a black—ah!—black altar.

DICKON A Druidical heirloom. His lordship's mother collects antiques.

RACHEL How fascinating!

RAVENSBANE Quite fascinating! On the walls hang pieces of iron.

DICKON Trophies of Saxon warfare.

RAVENSBANE And rusty horseshoes.

GENERAL MURMURS Horseshoes!

DICKON Presents from the German emperor. They were worn by the steeds of Charlemagne.

RAVENSBANE Quite so; and broken cart-wheels.

DICKON Reliques of British chariots.

RACHEL How mediæval it must be! [*To Justice Merton.*] And to think you never described it to us!

MISTRESS MERTON True, brother; you have been singularly reticent.

JUSTICE MERTON Permit me; it is impossible to report all one sees on one's travels.

MISTRESS MERTON Evidently.

RACHEL But surely your lordship's mother has other diversions besides collecting antiques. I have heard that in England ladies followed the hounds; and sometimes— [*Looking at her aunt and lowering her voice.*] they even dance.

RAVENSBANE Dance—ah, yes; my lady mother dances about the—the altar; she swings high a hammer.

DICKON Your lordship, your lordship! Pray, sir, check this vein of poetry. Lord Ravensbane symbolizes as a hammer and altar a golf-stick and tee—a Scottish game, which her ladyship plays on her Highland estates.

RICHARD [*To Mistress Merton.*] What do you think of this?

MISTRESS MERTON [*With a scandalized look toward her brother.*] He said to me "tush."

RICHARD [*To Justice Merton, indicating Dickon.*] Who is this magpie?

JUSTICE MERTON [*Hisses in fury.*] Satan!

RICHARD I beg pardon!

JUSTICE MERTON Satan, sir—makes you jealous.

RICHARD [*Bows stiffly.*] Good morning. [*Walking up to Ravensbane.*] Lord Ravensbane, I have a rustic colonial question to ask. Is it the latest fashion to smoke incessantly in ladies' parlours, or is it—mediæval?

DICKON His lordship's health, sir, necessitates—

RICHARD I addressed his lordship.

RAVENSBANE In the matter of fashions, sir— [*Hands his pipe to be refilled.*] My pipe, Dickon!

[*While Dickon holds his pipe—somewhat longer than usual—Ravensbane, with his mouth open as if about to speak, relapses into a vacant stare.*]

DICKON [*As he lights the pipe for Ravensbane, speaks suavely and low as if not to be overheard by him.*] Pardon me. The fact is, my young pupil is sensitive; the wound from his latest duel is not quite healed; you observe a slight lameness, an occasional absence of mind.

RACHEL A wound—in a real duel?

RICHARD Necessitates his smoking! A valid reason!

DICKON [*Aside.*] You, mistress, know the *true* reason—his lordship's heart.

RACHEL Believe me, sir—

RICHARD [*To Ravensbane, who is still staring vacantly into space.*] Well, well, your lordship. [*Ravensbane pays no attention.*] You were saying—? [*Dickon returns the pipe.*] in the matter of fashions, sir—?

RAVENSBANE [*Regaining slowly a look of intelligence, draws himself up with affronted hauteur.*] Permit me! [*Puffs several wreaths of smoke into the air.*] I *am* the fashions.

RICHARD [*Going.*] Insufferable! [*He pauses at the door.*]

MISTRESS MERTON [*To Justice Merton.*] Well—what do you think of that?

JUSTICE MERTON Spoken like King Charles himself.

MISTRESS MERTON Brother! brother! is there nothing wrong here?

JUSTICE MERTON Wrong, Cynthia! Manifestly you are quite ignorant of the manners of the great.

MISTRESS MERTON Oh, Gilead!

JUSTICE MERTON Where are you going?

MISTRESS MERTON To my room. [*Murmurs, as she hurries out.*] Dear! dear! if it should be that again!

[*Dickon and Justice Merton withdraw to a corner of the room.*]

RACHEL [*To Ravensbane.*] I—object to the smoke? Why, I think it is charming.

RICHARD [*Who has returned from the door, speaks in a low, constrained voice.*] Rachel!

RACHEL Oh!—you?

RICHARD You take quickly to European fashions.

RACHEL Yes? To what one in particular?

RICHARD Two; smoking and flirtation.

RACHEL Jealous?

RICHARD Of an idiot? I hope not. Manners differ, however. Your confidences to his lordship have evidently not included—your relation to me.

RACHEL Oh, our relations!

RICHARD Of course, since you wish him to continue in ignorance—

RACHEL Not at all. He shall know at once. Lord Ravensbane!

RAVENSBANE Fair mistress!

RICHARD Rachel, stop! I did not mean—

RACHEL [*To Ravensbane.*] My uncle did not introduce to you with sufficient elaboration this gentleman. Will you allow me to do so now?

RAVENSBANE I adore Mistress Rachel's elaborations.

RACHEL Lord Ravensbane, I beg to present Squire Talbot, *my betrothed.*

RAVENSBANE Betrothed! Is it— [*Noticing Richard's frown.*] is it pleasant?

RACHEL [*To Richard.*] Are you satisfied?

RICHARD [*Trembling with feeling.*] *More* than satisfied. [*Exit.*]

RAVENSBANE [*Looking after him.*] Ah! Betrothed is *not* pleasant.

RACHEL Not always.

RAVENSBANE [*Anxiously.*] Mistress Rachel is not pleased?

RACHEL [*Biting her lip, looks after Richard.*] With him.

RAVENSBANE Mistress Rachel will smile again?

RACHEL Soon.

RAVENSBANE [*Ardent.*] Ah! if she would only smile once more! What can Lord Ravensbane do to make her smile? See! will you puff my pipe? It is very pleasant. [*Offering the pipe.*]

RACHEL [*Smiling.*] Shall I try? [*Takes hold of it mischievously.*]

JUSTICE MERTON [*In a great voice.*] Rachel!

RACHEL Why, uncle!

JUSTICE MERTON [*From where he has been conversing in a corner with Dickon, approaches now and speaks suavely to Ravensbane.*] Permit me, your lordship— Rachel, you will kindly withdraw for a few moments; I desire to confer with Lord Ravensbane concerning his mother's—her ladyship's letter; [*Obsequiously to Dickon.*] —that is, if you think, sir, that your noble pupil is not too fatigued.

DICKON Not at all; I think his lordship will listen to you with much pleasure.

RAVENSBANE [*Bowing to Justice Merton, but looking at Rachel.*] With much pleasure.

DICKON And in the meantime, if Mistress Rachel will allow me, I will assist her in writing those invitations which your worship desires to send in her name.

JUSTICE MERTON Invitations—from my niece?

DICKON To his Excellency, the Lieutenant Governor; to your friends, the Reverend Masters at Harvard College, etc., etc.; in brief, to all your worship's select social acquaintance in the vicinity—to meet his lordship. It was so thoughtful in you to suggest it, sir, and believe me, his lordship appreciates your courtesy in arranging the reception in his honour for this afternoon.

RACHEL [*To Justice Merton.*] This afternoon! Are we really to give his lordship a reception this afternoon?

DICKON Your uncle has already given me the list of guests; so considerate! Permit me to act as your scribe, Mistress Rachel.

RACHEL With pleasure. [*To Justice Merton.*] And will it be here, uncle?

DICKON [*Looking at him narrowly.*] Your worship said *here*, I believe?

JUSTICE MERTON Quite so, sir; quite so, quite so.

DICKON [*Aside to Justice Merton.*] I advise nothing rash, Gilly; the brat has a weak heart.

RACHEL This way, Master Dickonson, to the study.

DICKON [*As he goes with Rachel.*] I will write and you sign?

RACHEL Thank you.

DICKON [*Aside, as he passes Ravensbane.*] Remember, Jack! Puff, puff!

RACHEL [*To Ravensbane, who stretches out his hand to her with a gesture of entreaty to stay.*] Your lordship is to be my guest. [*Courtesying.*] Till we meet again!

DICKON [*To Rachel.*] May I sharpen your quill? [*Exeunt.*]

RAVENSBANE [*Faintly, looking after her.*] Till—we—meet—again!

JUSTICE MERTON [*Low and vehement to Ravensbane.*] Impostor!

RAVENSBANE [*Still staring at the door.*] She is gone.

JUSTICE MERTON You at least shall not play the lord and master to my face.

RAVENSBANE Quite—gone!

JUSTICE MERTON I know with whom I have to deal. If I be any judge of my own flesh and blood—permit me—you shall quail before me.

RAVENSBANE [*Dejectedly.*] She did not smile— [*Joyously.*] She smiled!

JUSTICE MERTON Affected rogue! I know thee. I know thy feigned pauses, thy assumed vagaries. Speak; how much do you want?

RAVENSBANE Betrothed,—he went away. That was good. And then—she did not smile: that was not good. But then—she smiled! Ah! that was good.

JUSTICE MERTON Come back, coward, and face me.

RAVENSBANE First, the great sun shone over the corn-fields, the grass was green; the black wings rose and flew before me; then the door opened—and she looked at me.

JUSTICE MERTON Speak, I say! What sum? What treasure do you hope to bleed from me?

RAVENSBANE [*Ecstatically.*] Ah! Mistress Rachel!

JUSTICE MERTON Her! Scoundrel, if thou dost name her again, my innocent—my sweet maid! If thou dost—thou godless spawn of temptation—mark you, I will put an end—

[*Reaching for a pistol that rests in a rack on the wall,—the intervening form of Dickon suddenly appears, pockets the pistol, and exit.*]

DICKON I beg pardon; I forgot something.

JUSTICE MERTON [*Sinking into a chair.*] God is just. [*He holds his head in his hands and weeps.*]

RAVENSBANE [*For the first time, since Rachel's departure, observes Merton.*]

Permit me, sir, are you ill?

JUSTICE MERTON [*Recoiling.*] What art thou?

RAVENSBANE [*Monotonously.*]

I am Lord Ravensbane: Marquis of Oxford, Baron of Wittenberg, Elector of Worms, and—

JUSTICE MERTON And my son! [*Covers his face again.*]

RAVENSBANE [*Solicitously.*] Shall I call Dickon?

JUSTICE MERTON Yea, for thou art my son. The deed once done is never done, the past is the present.

RAVENSBANE [*Walking softly toward the door, calls.*] Dickon!

JUSTICE MERTON [*Starting up.*] No, do not call him. Stay, and be merciful. Tell me: I hate thee not; thou wast innocent. Tell me!—I thought thou hadst died as a babe.— Where has Dickon, our tyrant, kept thee these twenty years?

RAVENSBANE [*With gentle courtesy.*] Master Dickonson is my tutor.

JUSTICE MERTON And why has thy mother— Ah, I know well; I deserve all. But yet, it must not be published now! I am a justice now, an honoured citizen—and my young niece— Thy mother will not demand so much; she will be considerate; she will ask some gold, of course, but she will show pity!

RAVENSBANE My mother is the Marchioness of Rickby.

JUSTICE MERTON Yes, yes; 'twas well planned, a clever trick. 'Twas skilful of her. But surely thy mother gave thee commands to—

RAVENSBANE My mother gave me her blessing.

JUSTICE MERTON Ah, 'tis well then. Young man, my son, I too will give thee my blessing, if thou wilt but go—go instantly—go with half my fortune, go away forever, and leave my reputation unstained.

RAVENSBANE Go away? [*Starting for the study door.*] Ah, sir, with much pleasure.

JUSTICE MERTON You will go? You will leave me my honour—and my Rachel?

RAVENSBANE Rachel? Rachel is yours? No, no, Mistress Rachel is mine. We are ours.

JUSTICE MERTON [*Pleadingly.*] Consider the disgrace.

RAVENSBANE No, no; I have seen her eyes, they are mine; I have seen her smiles, they are mine; she is mine!

JUSTICE MERTON Consider, one moment consider—you, an illegitimate—and she—oh, think what thou art!

RAVENSBANE [*Monotonously, puffing smoke at the end.*] I am Lord Ravensbane: Marquis of Oxford, Baron of Wittenberg, Elector of Worms, and Count—

JUSTICE MERTON [*Wrenching the pipe from Ravensbane's hand and lips.*] Devil's child! Boor! Buffoon! [*Flinging the pipe away.*] I will stand thy insults no longer. If thou hast no heart—

RAVENSBANE [*Putting his hand to his side, staggers.*] Ah! my heart!

JUSTICE MERTON Hypocrite! Thou canst not fool me. I am thy father.

RAVENSBANE [*Faintly, stretching out his hand to him for support.*] Father!

JUSTICE MERTON Stand away. Thou mayst break thy heart and mine and the devil's, but thou shalt not break Rachel's.

RAVENSBANE [*Faintly.*] Mistress Rachel is mine— [*He staggers again, and falls, half reclining, upon a chair.*]

JUSTICE MERTON Good God! Can it be—his heart?

RAVENSBANE [*More faintly, beginning to change expression.*] Her eyes are mine; her smiles are mine. [*His eyes close.*]

JUSTICE MERTON [*With agitated swiftness, feels and listens at Ravensbane's side.*] Not a motion; not a sound! Yea, God, Thou art good! 'Tis his heart. He is—ah! he is my son. Judge Almighty, if he should die now; may I not be still a moment more and make sure. No, no, my son—he is changing. [*Calls.*] Help! Help! Rachel! Master Dickonson! Help! Richard! Cynthia! Come hither! [*Enter Dickon and Rachel.*]

RACHEL Uncle!

JUSTICE MERTON Bring wine. Lord Ravensbane has fainted.

RACHEL Oh! [*Turning swiftly to go.*] Micah, wine.

DICKON [*Detaining her.*] Stay! His pipe! Where is his lordship's pipe?

RACHEL Oh, terrible!

[*Enter, at different doors, Mistress Merton and Richard.*]

MISTRESS MERTON What's the matter?

JUSTICE MERTON [*To Rachel.*] He threw it away. He is worse. Bring the wine.

MISTRESS MERTON Look! How strange he appears

RACHEL [*Searching distractedly.*] The pipe! His lordship's pipe! It is lost, Master Dickonson.

DICKON [*Stooping, as if searching, with his back turned, having picked up the pipe, is filling and lighting it.*] It must be found. This is a heart attack, my friends; his lordship's life depends on the nicotine. [*Deftly he places the pipe in Rachel's way.*]

RACHEL Thank God! Here it is.

[*Carrying it to the prostrate form of Ravensbane, she lifts his head and is about to put the pipe in his mouth.*]

Shall I—shall I put it in?

RICHARD No! not you.

RACHEL Sir!

RICHARD Let his tutor perform that office.

RACHEL [*Lifting Lord Ravensbane's head again.*] Here, my lord.

RICHARD AND JUSTICE MERTON [*Together.*] Rachel!

RACHEL You, too, uncle?

DICKON Pardon me, Mistress Rachel; give the pipe at once. Only a token of true affection can revive his lordship now.

RICHARD [*As Rachel puts the pipe to Ravensbane's lips.*] I forbid it, Rachel.

RACHEL [*Watching only Ravensbane.*] My lord—my lord!

MISTRESS MERTON Give him air; unbutton his coat. [*Rachel unbuttons Ravensbane's coat, revealing the embroidered waistcoat.*] Ah, heavens! What do I see?

JUSTICE MERTON [*Looks, blanches, and signs silence to Mistress Merton.*] Cynthia!

DICKON See! He puffs—he revives. He is coming to himself.

MISTRESS MERTON [*Aside to Justice Merton, with deep tensity.*] That waistcoat! that waistcoat! Brother, hast thou never seen it before?

JUSTICE MERTON Never, my sister.

RACHEL [*As Ravensbane rises to his feet.*] At last!

DICKON Look! he is restored.

RACHEL God be thanked!

DICKON My lord, Mistress Rachel has saved your life.

RAVENSBANE [*Taking Rachel's hand.*] Mistress Rachel is mine; we are ours.

RICHARD Dare to repeat that.

RAVENSBANE [*Looking at Rachel.*] Her eyes are mine.

RICHARD [*Flinging his glove in his face.*] And that, sir, is yours. I believe such is the proper fashion in England. If your lordship's last duelling wound is sufficiently healed, perhaps you will deign a reply.

RACHEL Richard! Your lordship!

RAVENSBANE [*Stoops, picks up the glove, pockets it, bows to Rachel, and steps close to Richard.*] Permit me!

[*He blows a puff of smoke full in Richard's face.*]

ACT III

The same day. Late afternoon. The same scene as Act II.

RAVENSBANE *and* DICKON *discovered at table, on which are lying two flails. Ravensbane is dressed in a costume which, composed of silk and jewels, subtly approximates in design to that of his original grosser composition. So artfully, however, is this contrived that, to one ignorant of his origin, his dress would appear to be merely an odd personal whimsy; whereas, to one initiated, it would stamp him grotesquely as the apotheosis of scarecrows.*

Dickon is sitting in a pedagogical attitude; Ravensbane stands near him, making a profound bow in the opposite direction.

RAVENSBANE Believe me, ladies, with the true sincerity of the heart.

DICKON Inflection a little more lachrymose, please: "The *true* sincerity of the *heart*."

RAVENSBANE Believe me, ladies, with the *true* sincerity of the *heart*.

DICKON Prettily, prettily! Next!

RAVENSBANE [*Changing his mien, as if addressing another person.*] Verily, sir, as that prince of poets, the immortal Virgil, has remarked:

"Adeo in teneris consuescere multum est."

DICKON Hm! Act up to the sentiment.

RAVENSBANE Verily, sir, as that prince—

DICKON No, no; *basta*! The next.

RAVENSBANE [*With another change to courtly manner.*] Trust me, your Excellency, I will inform his Majesty of your courtesy.

DICKON His Majesty more emphatic. Remember! You must impress all of the guests this afternoon.

RAVENSBANE *His Majesty* of your courtesy.

DICKON Delicious! O thou exquisite flower of love! How thy natal composites have burst in bloom: The pumpkin in thee to a golden collarette; thy mop of crow's wings to these raven locks; thy broomstick to a lordly limp; thy corn-silk to these pale-tinted tassels. Verily in the gallery of scarecrows, thou art the Apollo Belvedere! But continue, Cobby dear: the retort now to the challenge.

RAVENSBANE [*With a superb air.*] The second, I believe.

DICKON Quite so, my lord.

RAVENSBANE Sir! The local person whom you represent has done himself the honour of submitting to me a challenge to mortal combat. Sir! Since the remotest times of my feudal ancestors, in such affairs of honour, choice of weapons has ever been the prerogative of the challenged. Sir! This right of etiquette must be observed. Nevertheless, believe me, I have no selfish desire that my superior attainments in this art should assume advantage over my challenger's ignorance. I have, therefore, chosen those combative utensils most appropriate both to his own humble origin and to local tradition. Permit me, sir, to reveal my choice. [*Pointing grandly to the table.*] There are my weapons

DICKON [*Clapping his hands.*] My darling *homunculus*! Thou shouldst have acted in Beaumont and Fletcher!

RAVENSBANE There are my weapons!

DICKON I could watch thy histrionics till midnight. But thou art tired, poor Jacky; two hours' rehearsal is fatiguing to your lordship.

RAVENSBANE Mistress Rachel—I may see her now?

DICKON Romeo! Romeo! Was ever such an amorous puppet show!

RAVENSBANE Mistress Rachel!

DICKON Wait; let me think! Thou art wound up now, my pretty apparatus, for at least six and thirty hours. The wooden angel Gabriel that trumpets the hours on the big clock in Venice is not a more punctual manikin than thou with my speeches. Thou shouldst run, therefore,—

RAVENSBANE [*Frowning darkly at Dickon.*] Stop talking; permit me! A tutor should know his place.

DICKON [*Rubbing his hands.*] Nay, your lordship is beyond comparison.

RAVENSBANE [*In a terrible voice.*] She will come? I shall see her? [*Enter* MICAH.]

MICAH Pardon, my lord.

RAVENSBANE [*Turning joyfully to Micah.*] Is it she?

MICAH Captain Bugby, my lord, the Governor's secretary.

DICKON Good. Squire Talbot's second. Show him in.

RAVENSBANE [*Flinging despairingly into a chair.*] Ah! ah

MICAH [*Lifting the flails from the table.*] Beg pardon, sir; shall I remove—

DICKON Drop them; go.

MICAH But, sir—

DICKON Go, thou slave! [*Exit Micah.*]

RAVENSBANE [*In childlike despair.*] She will not come! I shall not see her!

DICKON [*Handing him a book.*] Here, my lord; read. You must be found reading.

RAVENSBANE [*Flinging the book into the fireplace.*] She does not come!

DICKON Fie, fie, Jack; thou must not be breaking thy Dickon's apron-strings with a will of thine own. Come!

RAVENSBANE Mistress Rachel

DICKON Be good, boy, and thou shalt see her soon.

RAVENSBANE [*Brightening.*] I shall see her? [*Enter* CAPTAIN BUGBY.]

DICKON Your lordship was saying—Oh! Captain Bugby?

CAPTAIN BUGBY [*Nervous and awed.*] Captain Bugby, sir, ah! at Lord Ravensbane's service—ah!

DICKON I am Master Dickonson, his lordship's tutor.

CAPTAIN BUGBY Happy, sir.

DICKON [*To Ravensbane.*] My lord, this gentleman waits upon you from Squire Talbot. [*To Captain Bugby.*] In regard to the challenge of this morning, I presume?

CAPTAIN BUGBY The affair, ah! the affair of this morning, sir.

RAVENSBANE [*With his former superb air—to Captain Bugby.*] The second, I believe?

CAPTAIN BUGBY Quite so, my lord.

RAVENSBANE Sir! the local person whom you represent has done himself the honour of submitting to me a challenge to mortal combat. Sir! Since the remotest times of my feudal ancestors, in such affairs of honour, choice of weapons has ever been the prerogative of the challenged. Sir! this right of etiquette must be observed.

CAPTAIN BUGBY Indeed, yes, my lord.

DICKON Pray do not interrupt. [*To Ravensbane.*] Your lordship: "observed."

RAVENSBANE —observed. Nevertheless, believe me, I have no selfish desire that my superior attainments in this art should assume advantage over my challenger's ignorance. I have, therefore, chosen those combative utensils most appropriate both to his own humble origin and to local tradition. Permit me, sir, to reveal my choice. [*Pointing to the table.*] There are my weapons!

CAPTAIN BUGBY [*Looking, bewildered.*] These, my lord?

RAVENSBANE Those.

CAPTAIN BUGBY But these are—are flails.

RAVENSBANE Flails.

CAPTAIN BUGBY Flails, my lord?

RAVENSBANE There are my weapons.

CAPTAIN BUGBY Lord Ravensbane—I—ah! express myself ill—Do I understand that your lordship and Squire Talbot—

RAVENSBANE Exactly.

CAPTAIN BUGBY But your lordship—flails!

RAVENSBANE My adversary should be deft in their use. He has doubtless wielded them frequently on his barn floor.

CAPTAIN BUGBY Ahaha! I understand now. Your lordship—ah! is a wit. Haha! Flails!

DICKON His lordship's satire is poignant.

CAPTAIN BUGBY Indeed, sir, so keen that I must apologize for laughing at my principal's expense. [*Soberly to Ravensbane.*] My lord, if you will deign to speak one moment seriously—

RAVENSBANE Seriously?

CAPTAIN BUGBY I will take pleasure in informing Squire Talbot—ah! as to your *real* preference for—

RAVENSBANE For flails, sir. I have, permit me, nothing further to say. Flails are final. [*Turns away haughtily.*]

CAPTAIN BUGBY Must I really report to Squire Talbot—ah!—flails?

DICKON Lord Ravensbane's will is inflexible.

CAPTAIN BUGBY And his wit, sir, incomparable. I am sorry for the Squire, but 'twill be the greatest joke in years. Ah! will you tell me—is it— [*Indicating Ravensbane's smoking.*] is it the latest fashion?

DICKON Lord Ravensbane is always the latest.

CAPTAIN BUGBY Obliged servant, sir. Aha! Such a joke as—O lord! flails! [*Exit.*]

DICKON [*Returning to Ravensbane.*] Bravo, my pumpky dear! That squelches the jealous betrothed. Now nothing remains but for you to continue to dazzle the enamoured Rachel, and so present yourself to the Justice as a pseudo-son-nephew-in-law.

RAVENSBANE I may go to Mistress Rachel?

DICKON She will come to you. She is reading now a poem from you, which I left on her dressing-table.

RAVENSBANE She is reading a poem from me?

DICKON With your pardon, my lord, I penned it for you. I am something of a poetaster. Indeed, I flatter myself that I have dictated some of the finest lines in literature.

RAVENSBANE Dickon! She will come?

DICKON She comes! [*Enter* RACHEL, *reading from a piece of paper.*] Hush! Step aside; step aside first. Let her read it. [*Dickon draws Ravensbane back.*]

RACHEL Once more, [*Reads.*] "To Mistress R——, enchantress:

If faith in witchcraft be a sin, Alas! what peril he is in Who plights his faith and love in thee, Sweetest maid of sorcery.

If witchcraft be a whirling brain, A roving eye, a heart of pain, Whose wound no thread of fate can stitch, How hast thou conjured, cruel witch, With the brain, eye, heart, and total mortal residue of thine enamoured JACK LANTHORNE, [LORD R——."]

DICKON Now to leave the turtles alone. [*Exit.*]

RACHEL "To Mistress R——, enchantress:

If faith in witchcraft be—"

"To Mistress R——." R! It *must* be. R—— must mean—

RAVENSBANE [*With passionate deference.*] Rachel!

RACHEL Ah! How you surprised me, my lord.

RAVENSBANE You are come again; you are come again.

RACHEL Has anything happened? Tell me, my lord. Has Squire Talbot been here?

RAVENSBANE No, Mistress Rachel; not here.

RACHEL And you have not—Oh, my lord, I have been in such terror. But you are safe.—You have not fought?

RAVENSBANE No, Mistress Rachel; not fought.

RACHEL Thank God for that! But you will promise me—promise me that there shall be—no—duel!

RAVENSBANE I promise Mistress Rachel there shall be no duel.

RACHEL Your lordship is so good. You do not know how gratefully happy I am.

RAVENSBANE I know I am only a thing to make Mistress Rachel happy. Ah! look at me once more. When you look at me, I live.

RACHEL It is strange indeed, my lord, how the familiar world, the daylight the heavens themselves have changed since your arrival.

RAVENSBANE This is the world; this is the light; this is the heavens themselves. Mistress Rachel is looking at me.

RACHEL For me, it is less strange perhaps. I never saw a real lord before. But you, my lord, must have seen so many, many girls in the great world.

RAVENSBANE No, no; never.

RACHEL No other girls before to-day, my lord!

RAVENSBANE Before to-day? I do not know; I do not care. I was not here. To-day I was born—in your eyes. Ah! my brain whirls!

RACHEL [*Smiling.*] "If witchcraft be a whirling brain, A roving eye, a heart of pain,—" [*In a whisper.*] My lord, do you really believe in witchcraft?

RAVENSBANE With all my heart.

RACHEL And approve of it?

RAVENSBANE With all my soul.

RACHEL So do I—that is, innocent witchcraft; not to harm anybody, you know, but just to feel all the dark mystery and the trembling excitement—the way you feel when you blow out your candle all alone in your bedroom and watch the little smoke fade away in the moonshine.

RAVENSBANE Fade away in the moonshine!

RACHEL Oh, but we mustn't speak of it. In a town like this, all such mysticism is considered damnable. But your lordship understands and approves? I am so glad! Have you read the "Philosophical Considerations" of Glanville, the "*Saducismus Triumphatus*," and the "Presignifications of Dreams"? What kind of witchcraft, my lord, do you believe in?

RAVENSBANE In all yours.

RACHEL Nay, your lordship must not take me for a real witch. I can only tell fortunes, you know—like this morning.

RAVENSBANE I know; you told how my heart would break.

RACHEL Oh, that's palmistry, and that isn't always certain. But the surest way to prophesy—do you know what it is?

RAVENSBANE Tell me.

RACHEL To count the crows. Do you know how? One for sorrow—

RAVENSBANE Ha, yes!—Two for mirth!

RACHEL Three for a wedding—

RAVENSBANE Four for a birth—

RACHEL And five for the happiest thing on earth!

RAVENSBANE Mistress Rachel, come! Let us go and count five crows.

RACHEL [*Delightedly.*] Why, my lord, how did *you* ever learn it? I got it from an old goody here in town—a real witch-wife. If you will promise not to tell a secret, I will show you.—But you must promise!

RAVENSBANE I promise.

RACHEL Come, then. I will show you a real piece of witchcraft that I bought from her this morning—the glass of truth. There! Behind that curtain. If you look in, you will see—But come; I will show you. [*They put their hands on the cords of the curtain.*] Just pull that string, and—ah!

DICKON [*Stepping out through the curtain.*] Your pipe, my lord?

RACHEL Master Dickonson, how you frightened me!

DICKON So excessively sorry! I was observing the portrait of your uncle. I believe you were showing his lordship—

RACHEL [*Turning hurriedly away.*] Oh, nothing; nothing at all.

RAVENSBANE [*Sternly to Dickon.*] Why do you come?

DICKON [*Handing back Ravensbane's pipe filled.*] Allow me. [*Aside.*] 'Tis high time you came to the point, Jack; 'tis near your lordship's reception. Woo and win, boy; woo and win.

RAVENSBANE [*Haughtily.*] Leave me.

DICKON Your lordship's humble, very humble. [*Exit.*]

RACHEL [*Shivering.*] Oh! he is gone. My dear lord, why do you keep this man?

RAVENSBANE I—keep this man?

RACHEL I cannot—pardon my rudeness—I cannot endure him.

RAVENSBANE You do not like him? Ah, then, I do not like him also. We will send him away—you and I.

RACHEL You, my lord, of course; but I—

RAVENSBANE You will be Dickon! You will be with me always and light my pipe. And I will live for you, and fight for you, and kill your betrothed.

RACHEL [*Drawing away.*] No, no!

RAVENSBANE Ah! but your eyes say "yes." Mistress Rachel leaves me; but Rachel in her eyes remains. Is it not so?

RACHEL What can I say, my lord! It is true that since my eyes met yours, a new passion has entered into my soul. I have felt—your lordship will laugh at me—I have felt an inexpressible longing—but 'tis so impertinent, my lord, so absurd in me, a mere girl, and you a nobleman of power—yet I have felt it irresistibly, my dear lord,—a longing to help you. I am so sorry for you—so sorry for you! I pity you deeply.— Forgive me; forgive me, my lord!

RAVENSBANE It is enough.

RACHEL Indeed, indeed, 'tis so rude of me,—'tis so unreasonable.

RAVENSBANE It is enough. I grow—I grow—I grow! I am a plant; you give it rain and sun. I am a flower; you give it light and dew; I am a soul, you give it love and speech. I grow. Towards you—towards you I grow!

RACHEL My lord, I do not understand it, how so poor and mere a girl as I can have helped you. Yet I do believe it is so; for I feel it so. What can I do for you?

RAVENSBANE Do not leave me. Be mine. Let me be yours.

RACHEL Ah! but, my lord—do I love you?

RAVENSBANE What is "I love you"? Is it a kiss, a sigh, an embrace? Ah! then, you do not love me.—"I love you": is it to nourish, to nestle, to lift up, to smile upon, to make greater—a worm? Ah! then, you love me. [*Enter* RICHARD *at left back, unobserved.*]

RACHEL Do not speak so of yourself, my lord; nor exalt me so falsely.

RAVENSBANE Be mine.

RACHEL A great glory has descended upon this day.

RAVENSBANE Be mine.

RACHEL Could I but be sure that this glory is love—Oh, *then*! [*Turns toward Ravensbane.*]

RICHARD [*Stepping between them.*] It is *not* love; it is witchcraft.

RACHEL Who are you?—Richard?

RICHARD You have indeed forgotten me? Would to God, Rachel, I could forget you.

RAVENSBANE Sir, permit me—

RICHARD Silence! [*To Rachel.*] Against my will, I am a convert to your own mysticism; for nothing less than damnable illusion could so instantly wean your heart from me to—this. I do not pretend to understand it; but that it is witchcraft I am convinced; and I will save you from it.

RACHEL Go; please go.

RAVENSBANE Permit me, sir; you have not replied yet to flails!

RICHARD Permit *me*, sir. [*Taking something from his coat.*] My answer is—bare cob! [*Holding out a shelled corn-cob.*] Thresh this, sir, for your antagonist. 'Tis the only one worthy your lordship. [*Tosses it contemptuously towards him.*]

RAVENSBANE Upon my honour, as a man—

RICHARD As a *man* forsooth! Were you indeed a man, Lord Ravensbane, I would have accepted your weapons, and flailed you out of New England. But it is not my custom to chastise runagates from asylums, or to banter further words with a natural and a ninny.

RACHEL Squire Talbot! Will you leave my uncle's house?

RAVENSBANE One moment, mistress:—I did not wholly catch the import of this gentleman's speech, but I fancy I have insulted him by my reply to his challenge. One insult may perhaps be remedied by another. Sir, permit me to call you a ninny, and to offer you— [*Drawing his sword and offering it.*] swords.

RICHARD Thanks; I reject the offer.

RAVENSBANE [*Turning away despondently.*] He rejects it. Well!

RACHEL [*To Richard.*] And *now* will you leave?

RICHARD At once. But one word more. Rachel—Rachel, have you forgotten this morning and the glass of truth?

RACHEL [*Coldly.*] No.

RICHARD

Call it a fancy now if you will. I scoffed at it; yes. Yet *you* believed it. I loved you truly, you said. Well, have I changed?

RACHEL Yes.

RICHARD Will you test me again—in the glass?

RACHEL No. Go; leave us.

RICHARD I will go. I have still a word with your aunt.

RAVENSBANE [*To Richard.*] I beg your pardon, sir. You said just now that had I been a man—

RICHARD I say, Lord Ravensbane, that the straight fibre of a true man never warps the love of a woman. As for yourself, you have my contempt and pity. Pray to God, sir, pray to God to make you a man. [*Exit, right.*]

RACHEL Oh! it is intolerable! [*To Ravensbane.*] My dear lord, I do believe in my heart that I love you, and if so, I will with gratitude be your wife. But, my lord, strange glamours, strange darknesses reel, and bewilder my mind. I must be alone; I must think and decide. Will you give me this tassel?

RAVENSBANE [*Unfastening a silk tassel from his coat and giving it to her.*] Oh, take it.

RACHEL If I decide that I love you, that I will be your wife—I will wear it this afternoon at the reception. Good-by. [*Exit, right.*]

RAVENSBANE Mistress Rachel!— [*Solus.*] God, are you here? Dear God, I pray to you—make me to be a man! [*Exit, left.*]

DICKON [*Appearing in the centre of the room.*] Poor Jacky! Thou shouldst 'a' prayed to t'other one.

[*He disappears. Enter, right,* RICHARD *and* MISTRESS MERTON.]

MISTRESS MERTON [*Pointing to the wall.*] That is the portrait.

RICHARD Indeed! The design is very like.

MISTRESS MERTON 'Tis more than like, Richard; 'tis the very same. Two and twenty years ago she embroidered it for him, and he would insist on wearing it for the portrait he was then sitting for.

RICHARD That same Goody Rickby!

MISTRESS MERTON A pretty girl!—and a wild young man was my brother. The truth comes hard to tell thee, Richard; but he was wild, Gilead was wild. He told me the babe had died. But God worketh His own righteousness. Only—he must be saved now; Rachel must be saved; we must all be saved.

RICHARD You feel sure—very sure, Mistress Merton?

MISTRESS MERTON Yea, that waistcoat; 'tis the very one, I know it too well. And you see it accounts for all,—this silly impostor lord; my brother's strange patronage of him; the blackmail of this Master Dickonson—

RICHARD But who is *he*?

MISTRESS MERTON Nay, heaven knows! Some old crony perchance of Gilead's youth; some confederate of this woman Rickby.

RICHARD O God!—And Rachel sacrificed to these impostors; to an illegitimate—your brother would allow it!

MISTRESS MERTON Ah! but think of his own reputation, Richard. He a justice—the family honour!

RICHARD 'Tis enough. Well, and I must see this Goody Rickby, you think?

MISTRESS MERTON At once—at once. My brother has invited guests for this afternoon to meet "his lordship"! Return, if possible, before they come. She dwells at the blacksmith shop—you must buy her off. Oh, gold will buy her; 'tis the gold they're after—all of them; have her recall both these persons. [*Giving a purse.*] Take her that, Richard, and promise her more.

RICHARD [*Proudly.*] Keep it, Mistress Merton. I have enough gold, methinks, for my future wife's honour; or if not, I will earn it. [*Exit.*]

MISTRESS MERTON Richard! Ah, the dear lad, he should have taken it.

[*Enter* MICAH.]

MICAH The minister and his wife have turned into the gate, madam.

MISTRESS MERTON The guests! Is it so late?

MICAH Four o'clock, madam. [*Going to the table.*] Shall I remove these?

MISTRESS MERTON Flails! Flails in the parlour? Of course, remove them.

MICAH [*At the door.*] Madam, in all my past years of service at Merton House, I never waited upon a lord till to-day. Madam, in all my future years of service at Merton House, I trust I may never wait upon a lord again.

MISTRESS MERTON Micah, mind the knocker.

MICAH Yes, madam. [*Exit at left back. Sounds of a brass knocker outside.*]

MISTRESS MERTON Rachel! Rachel! [*Exit, right. Enter, left,* JUSTICE MERTON *and* DICKON.]

JUSTICE MERTON So you are contented with nothing less than the sacrifice of my niece?

DICKON Such a delightful room!

JUSTICE MERTON Are you merciless?

DICKON And such a living portrait of your worship! The waistcoat is so beautifully executed.

JUSTICE MERTON If I pay him ten thousand pounds— [*Enter* MICAH.]

MICAH Minister Dodge, your worship; and Mistress Dodge. [*Exit. Enter the* MINISTER *and his* WIFE.]

JUSTICE MERTON [*Stepping forward to receive them.*] Believe me, this is a great privilege.—Madam! [*Bowing.*]

MINISTER DODGE [*Taking his hand.*] The privilege is ours, Justice; to enter a righteous man's house is to stand, as it were, on God's threshold.

JUSTICE MERTON [*Nervously.*] Amen, amen. Permit me—ah! Lord Ravensbane, my young guest of honour, will be here directly—permit me to present his lordship's tutor, Master Dickonson; The Reverend Master Dodge, Mistress Dodge.

MINISTER DODGE [*Offering his hand.*] Master Dickonson, sir—

DICKON [*Barely touching the minister's fingers, bows charmingly to his wife.*] Madam, of all professions in the world, your husband's most allures me.

MISTRESS DODGE 'Tis a worthy one, sir.

DICKON Ah! Mistress Dodge, and so arduous—especially for a minister's wife. [*He leads her to a chair.*]

MISTRESS DODGE [*Accepting the chair.*] Thank you.

MINISTER DODGE Lord Ravensbane comes from abroad?

JUSTICE MERTON From London.

MINISTER DODGE An old friend of yours, I understand.

JUSTICE MERTON From London, yes. Did I say from London? Quite so; from London. [*Enter* MICAH.]

MICAH Captain Bugby, the Governor's secretary.

[*Exit. Enter* CAPTAIN BUGBY. *He walks with a slight lameness, and holds daintily in his hand a pipe, from which he puffs with dandy deliberation.*]

CAPTAIN BUGBY Justice Merton, your very humble servant.

JUSTICE MERTON Believe me, Captain Bugby.

CAPTAIN BUGBY [*Profusely.*] Ah, Master Dickonson! my dear friend Master Dickonson—this is indeed—ah! How is his lordship since—aha! but discretion! Mistress Dodge—her servant! Ah! yes, [*Indicating his pipe with a smile of satisfaction.*] the latest, I assure you; the very latest from London. Ask Master Dickonson.

MINISTER DODGE [*Looking at Captain Bugby.*] These will hatch out in the springtime.

CAPTAIN BUGBY [*Confidentially to Dickon.*] But really, my good friend, may not I venture to inquire how his lordship—ah! has been in health since the—ah! since—

DICKON [*Impressively.*] Oh! quite, quite!

[*Enter* MISTRESS MERTON; *she joins Justice Merton and Minister Dodge.*]

CAPTAIN BUGBY You know, I informed Squire Talbot of his lordship's epigrammatic retort—his retort of—shh! ha haha! Oh, that reply was a stiletto; 'twas sharper than a sword-thrust, I assure you. To have conceived it—'twas inspiration; but to have expressed it—oh! 'twas genius. Hush! "Flails!" Oh! It sticks me now in the ribs. I shall die with concealing it.

MINISTER DODGE [*To Mistress Merton.*] 'Tis true, mistress; but if there were more like your brother in the parish, the conscience of the community would be clearer.

[*Enter* MICAH.]

MICAH The Reverend Master Rand of Harvard College; the Reverend Master Todd of Harvard College.

[*Exit. Enter two elderly, straight-backed divines.*]

JUSTICE MERTON [*Greeting them.*] Permit me, gentlemen; this is fortunate—before your return to Cambridge.

[*He conducts them to Mistress Merton and Minister Dodge, centre. Seated left, Dickon is ingratiating himself with Mistress Dodge; Captain Bugby, laughed at by both parties, is received by neither.*]

CAPTAIN BUGBY [*Puffing smoke toward the ceiling.*] Really, I cannot understand what keeps his Excellency, the Lieutenant Governor, so long. He has two such charming daughters, Master Dickonson—

DICKON [*To Mistress Dodge.*] Yes, yes; such suspicious women with their charms are an insult to the virtuous ladies of the parish.

CAPTAIN BUGBY How, sir!

MISTRESS DODGE And to think that she should actually shoe horses herself!

DICKON It is too hard, dear Mistress Dodge; too hard!

MISTRESS DODGE You are so appreciative, Master Dickonson.

CAPTAIN BUGBY [*Piqued, walks another way.*] Well!

REV. MASTER RAND [*To Justice Merton.*] It would not be countenanced in the college yard, sir.

REV. MASTER TODD A pipe! Nay, *mores inhibitae!*

JUSTICE MERTON 'Tis most unfortunate, gentlemen; but I understand 'tis the new vogue in London. [*Enter* MICAH.]

MICAH His Excellency, Sir Charles Reddington, Lieutenant Governor; the Mistress Reddingtons.

CAPTAIN BUGBY At last!

MISTRESS MERTON [*Aside.*] Micah.

[*Micah goes to her. Enter* SIR CHARLES, MISTRESS REDDINGTON, *and* AMELIA REDDINGTON.]

JUSTICE MERTON Your Excellency, this is indeed a distinguished honour.

SIR CHARLES [*Shaking hands.*] Fine weather, Merton. Where's your young lord?

THE TWO GIRLS [*Courtesying.*] Justice Merton, Mistress Merton.

MICAH [*To Mistress Merton, as he is going out, right.*] I will speak to them, madam.

CAPTAIN BUGBY Oh, my dear Mistress Reddington! Charming Mistress Amelia! You are so very late, but you shall hear—hush!

MISTRESS REDDINGTON [*Noticing his pipe.*] Why, what is this, Captain?

CAPTAIN BUGBY Oh, the latest, I assure you, the very latest. Wait till you see his lordship.

AMELIA What! isn't he here? [*Laughing.*] La, Captain! Do look at the man!

CAPTAIN BUGBY Oh, he's coming directly. Quite the mode—what? Ah! but, ladies, you shall hear. [*He talks to them aside, where they titter.*]

SIR CHARLES [*To Dickon.*] What say? Travelling for his health?

DICKON Partially, your Excellency; but my young pupil and master is a singularly affectionate nature.

THE TWO GIRLS [*To Captain Bugby.*] What! flails—really! [*They burst into laughter among themselves.*]

DICKON He has journeyed here to Massachusetts peculiarly to pay this visit to Justice Merton—his father's dearest friend.

SIR CHARLES Ah! knew him abroad, eh?

DICKON In Rome, your Excellency.

MISTRESS DODGE [*To Justice Merton.*] Why, I thought it was in London.

JUSTICE MERTON London, true, quite so; we made a trip together to Lisbon—ah! Rome.

DICKON Paris, was it not, sir?

JUSTICE MERTON [*In great distress.*] Paris, Paris, very true; I am—I am—sometimes I am— [*Enter* MICAH, *right.*]

MICAH [*Announces.*] Lord Ravensbane. [*Enter right,* RAVENSBANE *with* RACHEL.]

JUSTICE MERTON [*With a gasp of relief.*] Ah! his lordship is arrived. [*Murmurs of "his lordship" and a flutter among the girls and Captain Bugby.*]

CAPTAIN BUGBY Look!—Now!

JUSTICE MERTON Welcome, my lord! [*To Sir Charles.*] Permit me, your Excellency, to introduce—

RAVENSBANE Permit me; Mistress Rachel will introduce—

RACHEL [*Courtesying.*] Sir Charles, allow me to present my friend, Lord Ravensbane.

MISTRESS REDDINGTON [*Aside to Amelia.*] Her *friend*—did you hear?

SIR CHARLES Mistress Rachel, I see you are as pretty as ever. Lord Ravensbane, your hand, sir.

RAVENSBANE Trust me, your Excellency, I will inform his Majesty of your courtesy.

CAPTAIN BUGBY [*Watching Ravensbane with chagrin.*] On my life! he's lost his limp.

RAVENSBANE [*Apart to Rachel.*] "A great glory has descended upon this day."

RACHEL [*Shyly.*] My lord!

RAVENSBANE Be sure—O mistress, be sure—that this glory is love.

SIR CHARLES [*Watching the two, whispers a loud aside to Justice Merton.*] Hoho! is it congratulations for your niece?

JUSTICE MERTON Not—not precisely.

DICKON [*Aside to Justice Merton.*] Why so, Gilly?

SIR CHARLES My daughters, Fanny and Amelia—Lord Ravensbane.

THE TWO GIRLS [*Courtesying.*] Your lordship!

SIR CHARLES Good girls, but silly.

THE TWO GIRLS Papa!

RAVENSBANE Believe me, ladies, with the *true* sincerity of the *heart*.

MISTRESS REDDINGTON Isn't he perfection!

CAPTAIN BUGBY What said I?

AMELIA [*Giggling.*] I can't help thinking of flails.

MISTRESS REDDINGTON Poor Squire Talbot! We must be nice to him now.

AMELIA Oh, especially *now*!

RAVENSBANE [*Whom Rachel continues to introduce to the guests; to Master Rand.*] Verily, sir, as that prince of poets, the immortal Virgil, has remarked: "Adeo in teneris consuescere multum est."

DICKON Just a word, your worship.

JUSTICE MERTON [*Going with him.*] Intolerable!

REV. MASTER TODD His lordship is evidently a university man.

REV. MASTER RAND Evidently most accomplished.

JUSTICE MERTON [*Aside to Dickon.*] A song! Why, it is beyond all bounds of custom and decorum.

DICKON Believe me, there is no such flatterer to win the maiden heart as music.

JUSTICE MERTON And here; in this presence! Never!

DICKON Nevertheless, it will amuse me vastly, and you will announce it.

RAVENSBANE [*To Minister Dodge.*] My opinion is simple: In such matters of church government, I am inclined toward the leniency of that excellent master, the Rev. John Wise, rather than the righteous obduracy of the Rev. Cotton Mather.

MINISTER DODGE Why, there, sir, I agree with you. [*Aside to his wife.*] How extremely well informed!

MISTRESS DODGE And so young, too!

JUSTICE MERTON [*With hesitant embarrassment, which he seeks to conceal.*] Your Excellency and friends, I have great pleasure in announcing his lordship's condescension in consenting to regale our present company—with a song.

SEVERAL VOICES [*In various degrees of amazement and curiosity.*] A song!

MISTRESS MERTON Gilead! What is this?

JUSTICE MERTON The selection is a German ballad—a particular favourite at the court of Prussia, where his lordship last rendered it. His tutor has made a translation which is entitled: "The Prognostication of the Crows," and I am requested to remind you that in the ancient heathen mythology of Germany, the crow or raven, was the fateful bird of the God Woden.

CAPTAIN BUGBY How prodigiously novel!

MINISTER DODGE [*Frowning.*] Unparalleled!

SIR CHARLES A ballad! Come now, that sounds like old England again. Let's have it. Will his lordship sing without music?

JUSTICE MERTON Master Dickonson, hem! has been—persuaded—to accompany his lordship on the virginals.

AMELIA How delightful!

REV. MASTER RAND [*Aside to Todd.*] Shall we remain?

REV. MASTER TODD We must.

RAVENSBANE [*To Rachel.*] My tassel, dear mistress; you do not wear it?

RACHEL My heart still wavers, my lord. But whilst you sing, I will decide.

RAVENSBANE Whilst I sing? My fate, then, is waiting at the end of a song?

RACHEL At the end of a song.

DICKON [*Touches Ravensbane's arm.*] Your lordship.

RAVENSBANE [*Starting, turns to the company.*] Permit me.

[*Dickon sits, facing left, at the virginals. At first, his fingers in playing give sound only to the soft tinkling notes of that ancient instrument; but gradually, strange notes and harmonies of an aërial orchestra mingle with, and at length drown, the virginals. The final chorus is produced solely by fantastic symphonic cawings, as of countless crows, in harsh but musical accord. During the song Richard enters. Dickon's music, however, does not cease but fills the intervals between the verses. To his accompaniment, amid the whispered and gradually increasing wonder, resentment, and dismay of the assembled guests, Ravensbane, with his eyes fixed upon Rachel, sings.*]

Baron von Rabenstod arose; (The golden sun was rising) Before him flew a flock of crows: Sing heigh! Sing heigh! Sing heigh! Sing—

"Ill speed, ill speed thee, baron-wight; Ill speed thy palfrey pawing! Blithe is the morn but black the night That hears a raven's cawing."

[*Chorus.*] Caw! Caw! Caw!

MISTRESS DODGE [*Whispers to her husband.*] Did you hear them?

MINISTER DODGE Hush!

AMELIA [*Sotto voce.*] What *can* it be?

CAPTAIN BUGBY Oh, the latest, be sure.

DICKON You note, my friends, the accompanying harmonics; they are an intrinsic part of the ballad, and may not be omitted.

RAVENSBANE [*Sings.*] The baron reckèd not a pin; (For the golden sun was rising) He rode to woo, he rode to win; Sing heigh! Sing heigh! Sing heigh! Sing— He rode into his prince's hall Through knights and damsels flow'ry: "Thy daughter, prince, I bid thee call; I claim her hand and dowry."

[*Enter Richard. Mistress Merton seizes his arm nervously.*]

MISTRESS MERTON [*Aside.*] Well?

RICHARD Gold will not buy her. She defies us.

SIR CHARLES [*To Captain Bugby.*] This gentleman's playing is rather ventriloquistical.

CAPTAIN BUGBY Quite, as it were.

REV. MASTER TODD This smells unholy.

REV. MASTER RAND [*To Todd.*] Shall we leave?

JUSTICE MERTON [*Sternly to Richard, who has attempted to talk with him aside.*] Not now.

RICHARD Pardon me—it *must* be now.

JUSTICE MERTON Squire Talbot—

RICHARD [*Very low.*] Sir—I come from Goody Rickby.

JUSTICE MERTON Hush! [*They go apart.*]

RAVENSBANE [*Sings.*] "What cock is this, with crest so high, That crows with such a pother?" "Baron von Rabenstod am I; Methinks we know each other." "Now welcome, welcome, dear guest of mine, So long why didst thou tarry? Now, for the sake of auld lang syne, My daughter thou shalt marry."

JUSTICE MERTON [*To Richard.*]

RICHARD What! you will sacrifice her?

JUSTICE MERTON What can I do?

RICHARD Tell her the truth at least.

JUSTICE MERTON Never, Richard, no, no, never that!

AMELIA [*To Bugby.*] And he kept right on smoking!

MINISTER DODGE [*Who, with Rand and Todd, has risen uneasily.*] This smacks of witchcraft.

REV. MASTER RAND The Justice seems moved.

RAVENSBANE [*Sings.*] The bride is brought, the priest as well; (The golden sun was passing) They stood beside the altar rail; Sing ah! Sing ah! Sing ah! Sing— "Woman, with this ring I thee wed." What makes his voice so awing? The baron by the bride is dead: Outside the crows were cawing.

Chorus. [*Which grows tumultuous, seeming to fill the room with the invisible birds.*] Caw! Caw! Caw!

[*The guests rise in confusion. Dickon still plays delightedly, and the strange music continues.*]

MINISTER DODGE This is no longer godly.—Justice Merton!

RICHARD [*To Justice Merton.*]

I told you, sir, that witchcraft, like murder, will out. If you want further proof, I believe I can provide it.

MINISTER DODGE Justice Merton, sir!

RAVENSBANE [*To Rachel, who holds his tassel in her hand.*] Ah! and you have my tassel!

RACHEL See! I will wear it now. You yourself shall fasten it.

RAVENSBANE Rachel! Mistress!

RACHEL My dear lord!

[*As Ravensbane is placing the silken tassel on Rachel's breast to fasten it there, Richard, by the mirror, pulls the curtain back.*]

RICHARD Lovers! This is the glass of truth. Behold yourselves!

RACHEL [*Looking into the glass, screams and turns her gaze fearfully upon Ravensbane.*] Ah! Do not look!

DICKON [*Who, having turned round from the virginals, has leapt forward, now turns back again, biting his finger.*] Too late! [*In the glass are reflected the figures of Rachel and Ravensbane—Rachel just as she herself appears, but Ravensbane in his essential form of a scarecrow, in every movement reflecting Ravensbane's motions. The thing in the glass is about to pin a wisp of corn-silk on the mirrored breast of the maiden.*]

RAVENSBANE What is there?

RACHEL [*Looking again, starts away from Ravensbane.*] Leave me! Leave me!— Richard!

RAVENSBANE [*Gazing at the glass, clings to Rachel as though to protect her.*] Help her! See! It is seizing her.

RACHEL Richard! [*She faints in Richard's arms.*]

RAVENSBANE Fear not, mistress, I will kill the thing. [*Drawing his sword, he rushes at the glass. Within, the scarecrow, with a drawn wheel-spoke, approaches him at equal speed. They come face to face and recoil.*] Ah! ah! fear'st thou me? What art thou? Why, 'tis a glass. Thou mockest me? Look, look, mistress, it mocks me! O God, no! no! Take it away. Dear God, do not look!—It is I!

ALL [*Rushing to the doors.*] Witchcraft! Witchcraft!

[*As Ravensbane stands frantically confronting his abject reflection, struck in a like posture of despair, the curtain falls.*]

ACT IV

The same. Night. The moon, shining in broadly at the window, discovers RAVENSBANE *alone, prostrate before the mirror. Raised on one arm to a half-sitting posture, he gazes fixedly at the vaguely seen image of the scarecrow prostrate in the glass.*

RAVENSBANE All have left me—but not thou. Rachel has left me; her eyes have turned away from me; she is gone. And with her, the great light itself from heaven has drawn her glorious skirts, contemptuous, from me—and they are gone together. Dickon, he too has left me—but not thou. All that I loved, all that loved me, have left me. A thousand ages—a thousand ages ago, they went away; and thou and I have gazed upon each other's desertedness. Speak! and be pitiful! If thou art I, inscrutable image, if thou dost feel these pangs thine own, show then self-mercy; speak! What art thou? What am I? Why are we here? How comes it that we feel and guess and suffer? Nay, though thou answer not these doubts, yet mock them, mock them aloud, even as there, monstrous, thou counterfeitest mine actions. Speak, abject enigma!—Ah! with what vacant horror it looks out and yearns toward me. Peace to thee! Thou poor delirious mute, prisoned in glass and moonlight, peace! Thou canst not escape thy gaol, nor I break in to thee. Poor shadow, thou—

[*Recoiling wildly.*]

Stand back, inanity! Thrust not thy mawkish face in pity toward me. Ape and idiot! Scarecrow!—to console me! Haha!—A flail and broomstick! a cob, a gourd and pumpkin, to fuse and sublimate themselves into a mage-philosopher, who puffeth metaphysics from a pipe and discourseth sweet philanthropy to itself—itself, God! Dost Thou hear? Itself! For even such am I—I whom Thou madest to love Rachel. Why, God—haha! dost Thou dwell in this thing? Is it Thou that peerest forth *at* me— *from* me? Why, hark then; Thou shalt listen, and answer—if Thou canst. Hark then, Spirit of life! Between the rise and setting of a sun, I have walked in this world of Thine. I have gazed upon it, I have peered within it, I have grown enamoured, enamoured of it. I have been thrilled with wonder, I have been calmed with knowledge, I have been exalted with sympathy. I have trembled with joy and passion. Power, beauty, love have ravished me. Infinity itself, like a dream, has blazed before me with the certitude of prophecy; and I have cried, "This world, the heavens, time itself, are mine to conquer," and I have thrust forth mine arm to wear Thy shield forever—and lo! for my shield Thou reachest me a mirror—and whisperest: "Know thyself! Thou art—a scarecrow: a tinkling clod, a rigmarole of dust, a lump of ordure, contemptible, superfluous, inane!" Haha! Hahaha! And with such scarecrows Thou dost people a planet! O ludicrous! Monstrous! Ludicrous! At least, I thank Thee, God! at least, this breathing bathos can laugh at itself. At least this hotch-potch nobleman of stubble is enough of an epicure to turn his own gorge. Thou hast vouchsafed to me, Spirit,—hahaha!—to know myself. Mine, mine is the consummation of man—even self-contempt!

[*Pointing in the glass with an agony of derision.*] Scarecrow! Scarecrow! Scarecrow!

THE IMAGE IN THE GLASS [*More and more faintly.*] Scarecrow! Scarecrow! Scarecrow!

[*Ravensbane throws himself prone upon the floor, beneath the window, sobbing. There is a pause of silence, and the moon shines brighter.—Slowly then Ravensbane, getting to his knees, looks out into the night.*]

RAVENSBANE What face are you, high up through the twinkling leaves? Why do you smile upon me with such white beneficence? Or why do you place your viewless hand upon my brow, and say, "Be comforted"? Do you not, like all the rest, turn, aghast, your eyes away from me—me, abject enormity, grovelling at your feet? Gracious being, do you not fear—despise me? To you alone am I not hateful—unredeemed? O white peace of the world, beneath your gaze the clouds glow silver, and the herded cattle, slumbering far afield, crouch—beautiful. The slough shines lustrous as a bridal veil. Beautiful face, you are Rachel's, and you have changed the world. Nothing is mean, but you have made it miraculous; nothing is loathsome, nothing ludicrous, but you have converted it to loveliness, that even this shadow of a mockery myself, cast by your light, gives me the dear assurance I am a man. Yea, more, that I too, steeped in your universal light, am beautiful. For you are Rachel, and you love me. You are Rachel in the sky, and the might of your serene loveliness has transformed me. Rachel, mistress, mother, beautiful spirit, out of my suffering you have brought forth my soul. I am saved!

THE IMAGE IN THE GLASS A very pretty sophistry.

[*The moonlight grows dimmer, as at the passing of a cloud.*]

RAVENSBANE Ah! what voice has snatched you from me?

THE IMAGE A most poetified pumpkin!

RAVENSBANE Thing! dost thou speak at last? My soul abhors thee.

THE IMAGE I *am* thy soul.

RAVENSBANE Thou liest.

THE IMAGE Our Daddy Dickon and our mother Rickby begot and conceived us at sunrise, in a Jack-o'-lantern.

RAVENSBANE Thou liest, torturing illusion. Thou art but a phantom in a glass.

THE IMAGE Why, very true. So art thou. *We* are a pretty phantom in a glass.

RAVENSBANE It is a lie. I am no longer thou. I feel it; I am a man.

THE IMAGE And prithee, what's a man? Man's but a mirror, Wherein the imps and angels play charades, Make faces, mope, and pull each other's hair— Till crack! the sly urchin Death shivers the glass, And the bare coffin boards show underneath.

RAVENSBANE Yea! if it be so, thou coggery! if both of us be indeed but illusions, why, now let us end together. But if it be not so, then let *me* for evermore be free of thee. Now is the test—the glass! [*Springing to the fireplace, he seizes an iron cross-piece from the andirons.*] I'll play your urchin Death and shatter it. Let see what shall survive! [*He rushes to strike the glass with the iron.* DICKON *steps out of the mirror, closing the curtain.*]

DICKON I wouldn't, really!

RAVENSBANE Dickon! dear Dickon! is it you?

DICKON Yes, Jacky! it's dear Dickon, and I really wouldn't.

RAVENSBANE Wouldn't what, Dickon?

DICKON Sweep the cobwebs off the sky with thine aspiring broomstick. When a man questions fate, 'tis bad digestion. When a scarecrow does it, 'tis bad taste.

RAVENSBANE At last, *you* will tell me the truth, Dickon! Am I then—that thing?

DICKON You mustn't be so sceptical. Of course you're that thing.

RAVENSBANE Ah me despicable! Rachel, why didst thou ever look upon me?

DICKON I fear, cobby, thou hast never studied woman's heart and hero-worship. Take thyself now. I remarked to Goody Bess, thy mother, this morning, as I was chucking her thy pate from the hay-loft, that thou wouldst make a Mark Antony or an Alexander before night.

RAVENSBANE Thou, then, didst create me!

DICKON [*Bowing.*] Appreciate the honour. Your lordship was designed for a corn-field; but I discerned nobler potentialities: the courts of Europe and Justice Merton's *salon.* In brief, your lordship's origins were pastoral, like King David's.

RAVENSBANE Cease! cease! in pity's name. You do not know the agony of being ridiculous.

DICKON Nay, Jacky, all mortals are ridiculous. Like you, they were rummaged out of the muck; and like you, they shall return to the dunghill. I advise 'em, like you, to enjoy the interim, and smoke.

RAVENSBANE This pipe, this ludicrous pipe that I forever set to my lips and puff! Why must I, Dickon? Why?

DICKON To avoid extinction—merely. You see, 'tis just as your fellow in there [*Pointing to the glass.*] explained. You yourself are the subtlest of mirrors, polished out of pumpkin and pipe-smoke. Into this mirror the fair Mistress Rachel has projected her lovely image, and thus provided you with what men call a soul.

RAVENSBANE Ah! then, I have a soul—the truth of me? Mistress Rachel has indeed made me a man?

DICKON Don't flatter thyself, cobby. Break thy pipe, and whiff—soul, Mistress Rachel, man, truth, and this pretty world itself, go up in the last smoke.

RAVENSBANE No, no! not Mistress Rachel—for she is beautiful; and the images of beauty are immutable. She told me so.

DICKON What a Platonic young lady! Nevertheless, believe me, Mistress Rachel exists for your lordship merely in your lordship's pipe-bowl.

RAVENSBANE Wretched, niggling caricature that I am! All is lost to me—all!

DICKON "Paradise Lost" again! Always blaming it on me. There's that gaunt fellow in England has lately wrote a parody on me when I was in the apple business.

RAVENSBANE [*Falling on his knees and bowing his head.*] O God! I am so contemptible!

[*Enter, at door back,* GOODY RICKBY; *her blacksmith garb is hidden under a dingy black mantle with peaked hood.*]

DICKON Good verse, too, for a parody! [*Ruminating, raises one arm rhetorically above Ravensbane.*]

"Farewell, happy fields Where joy forever dwells! Hail, horrors; hail, Infernal world! and thou, profoundest Hell, Receive thy new possessor."

GOODY RICKBY [*Seizing his arm.*] Dickon!

DICKON Hullo! You, Bess!

GOODY RICKBY There's not a minute to lose. Justice Merton and the neighbours have ended their conference at Minister Dodge's, and are returning here.

DICKON What! coming back in the dark? They ran away in the daylight as if the ghosts were after 'em.

GOODY RICKBY [*At the window.*] I see their lanterns down the road.

DICKON Well, let 'em come. We're ready.

GOODY RICKBY But thou toldst me they had discovered—

DICKON A scarecrow in a mirror. Well? The glass is bewitched; that's all.

GOODY RICKBY All? Witchcraft is hanging—that's all! Come, how shall the mirror help us?

DICKON 'Tis very simple. The glass is bewitched. Mistress Rachel—mind you—shall admit it. She bought it of you.

GOODY RICKBY Yea, of me; 'twill be me they'll hang.

DICKON Good! then the glass is bewitched. The glass bewitches the room; for witchcraft is catching and spreads like the small-pox. *Ergo*, the distorted image of Lord Ravensbane; *ergo*, the magical accompaniments of the ballad; *ergo*, the excited fancies of all the persons in the room. *Ergo*, the glass must needs be destroyed, and the room thoroughly disinfected by the Holy Scriptures. *Ergo*, Master Dickonson himself reads the Bible aloud, the guests apologize and go home, the Justice squirms again in his merry dead past, and his fair niece is wed to the pumpkin.

RAVENSBANE Hideous! Hideous!

GOODY RICKBY Your grateful servant, Devil! But the mirror was bought of me—of me, the witch. Wilt thou be my hangman, Dickon?

DICKON Wilt thou give me a kiss, Goody? When did ever thy Dickon desert thee?

GOODY RICKBY But how, boy, wilt thou—

DICKON Trust me, and thy son. When the Justice's niece is thy daughter-in-law, all will be safe. For the Justice will cherish his niece's family.

GOODY RICKBY But when he knows—

DICKON But he shall *not* know. How can he? When the glass is denounced as fraudulent, how will he, or any person, ever know that we made this fellow out of rubbish? Who, forsooth, but a poet—or a devil—*would* believe it? You mustn't credit men with our imaginations, my dear.

RAVENSBANE Mockery! Always mockery!

GOODY RICKBY Then thou wilt pull me through this safe?

DICKON As I adore thee—and my own reputation.

GOODY RICKBY [*Hurrying away.*] Till we meet, then, boy.

DICKON Stay, marchioness—his lordship!

GOODY RICKBY [*Turning.*] His lordship's pardon! How fares "the bottom of thy heart," my son?

DICKON My lord—your lady mother.

RAVENSBANE Begone, woman.

GOODY RICKBY [*Courtesying, laughs shrilly.*] Your servant—my son! [*About to depart.*]

RAVENSBANE Ye lie! Both of you! Ye lie—I was born of Rachel.

DICKON Tut, tut, Jacky; you mustn't mix up mothers and prospective wives at your age. It's fatal.

GOODY RICKBY [*Excitedly.*] They're coming! [*Exit.*]

DICKON [*Calling after her.*] Fear not; if thou shouldst be followed, I will overtake thee.

RAVENSBANE She is coming; Rachel is coming, and I may not look upon her!

DICKON Eh? Why not?

RAVENSBANE I am a monster.

DICKON And born of her—Fie! fie!

RAVENSBANE O God! I know not; I mock myself; I know not what to think. But this I know, I love Rachel. I love her, I love her.

DICKON And shalt have her.

RAVENSBANE Have her, Dickon?

DICKON For lover and wife.

RAVENSBANE For wife?

DICKON For wife and all. Thou hast but to obey.

RAVENSBANE Ah! who will do this for me?

DICKON I!

RAVENSBANE Dickon! Wilt make me a man—a man and worthy of her?

DICKON Fiddlededee! I make over no masterpieces. Thy mistress shall be Cinderella, and drive to her palace with her gilded pumpkin.

RAVENSBANE It is the end.

DICKON What! You'll not?

RAVENSBANE Never.

DICKON Harkee, manikin. Hast thou learned to suffer?

RAVENSBANE [*Wringing his hands.*] O God!

DICKON *I* taught thee. Shall I teach thee further?

RAVENSBANE Thou canst not.

DICKON Cannot—ha! What if I should teach Rachel too?

RAVENSBANE Rachel!—Ah! now I know thee.

DICKON [*Bowing.*] Flattered.

RAVENSBANE Devil! Thou wouldst not torment Rachel?

DICKON Not if my lord—

RAVENSBANE Speak! What must I do?

DICKON *Not* speak. Be silent, my lord, and acquiesce to all I say.

RAVENSBANE I will be silent.

DICKON And acquiesce?

RAVENSBANE I will be silent.

[*Enter* MINISTER DODGE, *accompanied by* SIR CHARLES REDDINGTON, CAPTAIN BUGBY, *the* REV. MASTERS RAND *and* TODD, *and followed by* JUSTICE MERTON, RICHARD, MISTRESS MERTON, *and* RACHEL. *Richard and Rachel stand somewhat apart, Rachel drawing close to Richard and hiding her face. All wear their outer wraps, and two or three hold lanterns, which, save the moon, throw the only light upon the scene. All enter solemn and silent.*]

MINISTER DODGE Lord, be Thou present with us, in this unholy spot.

SEVERAL MEN'S VOICES Amen.

DICKON Friends! Have you seized her? Is she made prisoner?

MINISTER DODGE Stand from us.

DICKON Sir, the witch! Surely you did not let her escape?

ALL The witch!

DICKON A dame in a peaked hood. She has but now fled the house. She called herself—Goody Rickby.

ALL Goody Rickby!

MISTRESS MERTON She here!

DICKON Yea, mistress, and hath confessed all the damnable art, by which all of us have lately been so terrorized, and his lordship, my poor master, so maligned and victimized.

RICHARD Victimized!

JUSTICE MERTON What confessed she?

MINISTER DODGE What said she?

DICKON This: It appeareth that, for some time past, she hath cherished revengeful thoughts against our honoured host, Justice Merton.

JUSTICE MERTON Sir! What cause—what cause—

DICKON Inasmuch as your worship hath ever so righteously condemned her damnable faults, and threatened them punishment.

MINISTER DODGE Yea—well?

DICKON Thus, in revenge, she bewitched yonder mirror, and this very morning unlawfully inveigled this sweet young lady into purchasing it.

SIR CHARLES Mistress Rachel!

MINISTER DODGE [*To Rachel.*] Didst thou purchase that glass?

RACHEL [*In a low voice.*] Yes.

MINISTER DODGE From Goody Rickby?

RACHEL Yes.

RICHARD Sir—the blame was mine.

RACHEL [*Clinging to him.*] O Richard!

DICKON Pardon, my friends. The fault rests upon no one here. The witch alone is to blame. Her black art inveigled this innocent maid into purchasing the glass; her black art bewitched this room and all that it contained—even to these innocent virginals, on which I played.

MINISTER DODGE Verily, this would seem to account—but the image; the damnable image in the glass?

DICKON A familiar devil of hers—a sly imp, it seems, who wears to mortal eyes the shape of a scarecrow. 'Twas he, by means of whom she bedevilled this glass, by making it his *habitat*. When, therefore, she learned that honour and happiness were yours, Justice Merton, in the prospect of Lord Ravensbane as your nephew-in-law, she commanded this devil to reveal himself in the glass as my lord's own image, that thus she might wreck your family felicity.

MINISTER DODGE Infamous!

DICKON Indeed, sir, it was this very devil whom but now she stole here to consult withal, when she encountered me, attendant here upon my poor prostrate lord, and— held by the wrath in my eye—confessed it all.

SIR CHARLES Thunder and brimstone! Where is this accursed hag?

DICKON Alas—gone, gone! If you had but stopped her.

MINISTER DODGE I know her den—the blacksmith shop.

SIR CHARLES [*Starting.*] Which way?

MINISTER DODGE To the left.

SIR CHARLES Go on, there.

MINISTER DODGE My honoured friend, we shall return and officially destroy this fatal glass. But first, we must secure the witch. Heaven shield, with her guilt, the innocent!

THE MEN [*As they hurry out.*] Amen.

SIR CHARLES [*Outside.*] Go on!

[*Exeunt all but Richard, Rachel, Justice Merton, Mistress Merton, Dickon, and Ravensbane.*]

DICKON [*To Justice Merton, who has importuned him, aside.*] And reveal thy youthful escapades to Rachel?

JUSTICE MERTON God help me! no.

DICKON So then, dear friends, this strange incident is happily elucidated. The pain and contumely have fallen most heavily upon my dear lord and master, but you are witnesses, even now, of his silent and Christian forgiveness of your suspicions. Bygones, therefore, be bygones. The future brightens—with orange-blossoms! Hymen and Felicity stand with us here ready to unite two amorous and bashful lovers. His lordship is reticent; yet to you alone, of all beautiful ladies, Mistress Rachel—

RAVENSBANE [*In a mighty voice.*] Silence!

DICKON My lord would—

RAVENSBANE Silence! Dare not to speak to her!

DICKON [*Biting his lip.*] My babe is weaned.

RACHEL [*Still at Richard's side.*] Oh, my lord, if I have made you suffer—

RICHARD [*Appealingly.*] Rachel!

RAVENSBANE [*Approaching her, raises one arm to screen his face.*] Gracious lady! let fall your eyes; look not upon me. If I have dared remain in your presence, if I dare now speak once more to you, 'tis because I would have you know—O forgive me!— that I love you.

RICHARD Sir! This lady has renewed her promise to be my wife.

RAVENSBANE Your wife, or not, I love her.

RICHARD Zounds!

RAVENSBANE Forbear, and hear me! For one wonderful day I have gazed upon this, your world. The sun has kindled me and the moon has blessed me. A million forms—of trees, of stones, of stars, of men, of common things—have swum like motes before my eyes; but one alone was wholly beautiful. That form was Rachel: to her alone I was not ludicrous; to her I also was beautiful. Therefore, I love her. You talk to me of mothers, mistresses, lovers, and wives and sisters, and you say men love these. What is love? The sun's enkindling and the moon's quiescence; the night and day of the world—the *all* of life, the all which must include both you and me and God, of whom you dream. Well then, I love you, Rachel. What shall prevent me? Mistress, mother, wife—thou art all to me!

RICHARD My lord, I can only reply for Mistress Rachel, that you speak like one who does not understand this world.

RAVENSBANE O God! Sir, and do you? If so, tell me—tell me before it be too late—why, in this world, such a thing as *I* can love and talk of love. Why, in this world, a true man and woman, like you and your betrothed, can look upon this counterfeit and be deceived.

RACHEL AND RICHARD Counterfeit?

RAVENSBANE Me—on me—the ignominy of the earth, the laughing-stock of the angels!

RACHEL Why, my lord. Are you not—

RAVENSBANE No.

JUSTICE MERTON [*To Ravensbane.*] Forbear! Not to her—

DICKON My lord forgets.

RACHEL Are you not Lord Ravensbane?

RAVENSBANE Marquis of Oxford, Baron of Wittenberg, Elector of Worms, and Count of Cordova? No, I am *not* Lord Ravensbane. I am Lord Scarecrow! [*He bursts into laughter.*]

RACHEL [*Shrinking back.*] Ah me!

RAVENSBANE A nobleman of husks, bewitched from a pumpkin.

RACHEL The image in the glass was true?

RAVENSBANE Yes, true. It is the glass of truth—thank God! Thank God for you, dear.

JUSTICE MERTON Richard! Go for the minister; this proof of witchcraft needs be known. [*Richard does not move.*]

DICKON My lord, this grotesque absurdity must end.

RAVENSBANE True, Dickon! This grotesque absurdity must end. The laugher and the laughing-stock, man and the worm, possess at least one dignity in common: both must die.

DICKON [*Speaking low.*] Remember! if you dare—Rachel shall suffer for it.

RAVENSBANE You lie. She is above your power.

DICKON Still, thou darest not—

RAVENSBANE Fool, I dare. [*Turning to Rachel.*] Mistress, this pipe is I. This intermittent smoke holds, in its nebula, Venus, Mars, the world. If I should break it—Chaos and the dark! And this of me that now stands up will sink jumbled upon the floor—a scarecrow. See! I break it.

[*He breaks the pipe in his hands, and flings the pieces at Dickon's feet in defiance; then turns, agonized, to Rachel.*] Oh, Rachel, could I have been a man—!

DICKON [*Picking up the pieces of pipe, turns to Rachel.*] Mademoiselle, I felicitate you; you have outwitted the devil. [*Kissing his fingers to her, he disappears.*]

MISTRESS MERTON [*Seizing the Justice's arm in fright.*] Satan!

JUSTICE MERTON [*Whispers.*] Gone!

RACHEL Richard! Richard! support him.

RICHARD [*Sustaining Ravensbane, who sways.*] He is fainting. A chair!

RACHEL [*Placing a chair, helps Richard to support Ravensbane toward it.*] How pale; but yet no change.

RICHARD His heart, perhaps.

RACHEL Oh, Dick, if it should be some strange mistake! Look! he is noble still. My lord! my lord! the glass—

[*She draws the curtain of the mirror, just opposite which Ravensbane has sunk into the chair. At her cry, he starts up faintly and gazes at his reflection, which is seen to be a normal image of himself.*]

RAVENSBANE Who is it?

RACHEL Yourself, my lord—'tis the glass of truth.

RAVENSBANE [*His face lighting with an exalted joy, starts to his feet, erect, before the glass.*] A man! [*He falls back into the arms of the two lovers.*] Rachel! [*He dies.*]

RACHEL Richard, I am afraid. Was it a chimera, or a hero?

FINIS

Lector House believes that a society develops through a two-fold approach of continuous learning and adaptation, which is derived from the study of classic literary works spread across the historic timeline of literature records. Therefore, we aim at reviving, repairing and redeveloping all those inaccessible or damaged but historically as well as culturally important literature across subjects so that the future generations may have an opportunity to study and learn from past works to embark upon a journey of creating a better future.

This book is a result of an effort made by Lector House towards making a contribution to the preservation and repair of original ancient works which might hold historical significance to the approach of continuous learning across subjects.

HAPPY READING & LEARNING!

LECTOR HOUSE LLP
E-MAIL: lectorpublishing@gmail.com

www.ingramcontent.com/pod-product-compliance
Lightning Source LLC
LaVergne TN
LVHW091526170726
843492LV00004B/1076